DEMONOLOGY
OF THE
EARLY
CHRISTIAN WORLD

Everett Ferguson

Symposium Series
Volume 12

The Edwin Mellen Press
New York and Toronto

Library of Congress Cataloging In Publication Data

Ferguson, Everett, 1933-
    Demonology of the early Christian world.

    Lectures presented at the University of Mississippi,
Oxford, Miss., Feb. 15-17, 1980.
    Bibliography: p.
    Includes index.
    1. Demonology--Biblical teaching--Addresses, essays,
lectures. 2. Demonology--History of doctrines--Early
church, ca. 30-600--Addresses, essays, lectures.
3. Demonology--Rome--Addresses, essays, lectures.
4. Bible. N.T.--Criticism, interpretation, etc.--
Addresses, essays, lectures. I. Title.
BS2545.D5F47 1984   235'.4.09015   84-16681
ISBN 0-88946-703-X

Symposium Series
Series ISBN 0-88496-989-X

The Edwin Mellen Press
P.O. Box 450
Lewiston, New York 14092

Printed in the United States of America

TO

Christian students, teachers, and ministers who serve their Lord in the context of a secular campus.

CONTENTS

PREFACE

These lectures were given at the University Christian Student Center, University of Mississippi, Oxford, Mississippi, on February 15-17, 1980. In preparing them for publication I have made few changes from the form in which they were delivered. Some account is taken in the notes of studies which have appeared since the lectures were prepared. My purpose in the lectures is largely historical and descriptive. It is hoped that this presentation will make more accessible the comparative source material which will make the Biblical references to demons more understandable. Contemporary phenomena are not considered, as being outside my competence; but those with that interest should find here much that will be helpful in evaluating modern reports. My own perspective is expressed in the fifth lecture (chapter), where the New Testament attitude toward all claims opposed to the exclusive lordship of Jesus Christ is presented.

I wish to express my gratitude to the University Christian Student Center and in particular Professor Douglas Shields for hospitality and interest in these lectures, to Abilene Christian University for encouragement in various ways of my studies, and to Herbert Richardson and the Edwin Mellen Press for acceptance of these lectures into the Symposium Series.

Everett Ferguson

Abilene Christian University

DEMONOLOGY
OF THE
EARLY
CHRISTIAN WORLD

CHAPTER I

JESUS AND THE DEMONS

Then they arrived at the country of the
Gerasenes, which is opposite Galilee. And
as [Jesus] stepped out on land, there met
him a man from the city who had demons; for
a long time he had worn no clothes, and he
lived not in a house but among the tombs.
When he saw Jesus, he cried out and fell
down before him, and said with a loud voice,
"What have you to do with me, Jesus, Son of
the Most High God? I beseech you, do not
torment me." For he had commanded the unclean spirit to come out of the man. (For
many a time it had seized him; he was kept
under guard, and bound with chains and
fetters, but he broke the bonds and was
driven by the demon into the desert.)
Jesus then asked him, "What is your name?"
And he said, "Legion"; for many demons had
entered him. And they begged him not to
command them to depart into the abyss. Now
a large herd of swine was feeding there on
the hillside; and they begged him to let
them enter these. So he gave them leave.
Then the demons came out of the man and
entered the swine, and the herd rushed down
the steep bank into the lake and were
drowned.

When the herdsmen saw what had happened,
they fled, and told it in the city and in
the country. Then people went out to see
what had happened, and they came to Jesus,
and found the man from whom the demons had
gone, sitting at the feet of Jesus, clothed
and in his right mind; and they were afraid.
And those who had seen it told them how he
who had been possessed with demons was
healed. Then all the people of the
surrounding country of the Gerasenes asked
him to depart from them; for they were
seized with great fear; so he got into the
boat and returned. The man from whom the
demons had gone begged that he might be

with him; but he sent him away, saying,
"Return to your home, and declare how much
God has done for you." And he went away,
proclaiming throughout the whole city how
much Jesus had done for him. (Luke 8:
26-39)

This is one of the most astonishing stories
in the Gospels. I have quoted the Gospel
according to Luke, but the same account is found
also in Matthew and Mark.[1] The story highlights
the conflict between Jesus and the demons, a
conflict which occupied a prominent place in
Jesus' ministry.

The story of the Gerasene demoniac contains
elements which reflect the popular demonology of
Jesus' day. These elements will find further
illustration as we proceed with this study of
Jesus' encounters with the demons and especially
in succeeding studies of the surrounding world
in which Jesus lived. We may mention now some
of those common elements: Demons haunted
deserted areas (this poor victim "was driven by
the demon into the desert"--Luke 8:29),[2] and
they lived in cemeteries (Legion lived "not in a
house but among the tombs"--Luke 8:27).[3] Demons
could take possession of a person, who showed
signs of insanity because a different personality dwelled in him (the demon "seized him" and
drove him--Luke 8:29; the demon spoke separately
from the man--Luke 8:28, 31; and there was a
dramatic difference in behavior before and after
the cure--contrast the nakedness and violent,

restless movement in Luke 8:27, 29 with sitting
clothed and in his right mind in Luke 8:35).[4]
The demon gave abnormal abilities to the person
possessed (in this case unusual strength--he
broke chains and fetters--Luke 8:29).[5] The knowledge of the name gave control over the person
(his name was Legion--Luke 8:30).[6] It was possible to expel the demon or (in this case) demons
(Luke 8:29, 31, 33).[7] And the demons could go
from a human being into animals (the unclean
spirits entered the herd of unclean animals and
caused the same violent, uncontrolled behavior
they had in the man and caused them to run down
a steep bank into the lake where they drowned--
Luke 8:33).[8] The destiny of the demons is the
abyss (Luke 8:31).[9]

Our purpose at the present is not to dwell
on these features, for although interesting in
various ways, I consider them less important than
some other aspects of Jesus' encounter with the
demonic. There are also some distinctive elements in this story, and some particularly Christian elements; and to these we will pay more
attention. Our method of approach will be to
examine other accounts of Jesus' dealings with
demons and notice what teaching in regard to
demons emerges from a comparison of these
accounts. I have chosen to follow the accounts
in Luke.[10] Luke has more references to demons
than either of the other Gospels, and he is
somewhat fuller in some of the accounts which he

shares in common with Matthew and Mark. But the
demons are prominent in Matthew and Mark, as
well, and we shall draw passages from them to
fill out the discussion.

Jesus' Ministry: Demons and Illness

As preliminary to this examination of particular incidents involving Jesus and demons, I
would like to note that in the summaries of Jesus'
ministry by the various gospel writers the casting out of demons is often mentioned. This shows
that it was a prominent activity by Jesus. Thus
Mark 1:39 says, "And he went throughout all
Galilee, preaching in their synagogues and casting out demons." Luke's summary, rather typ-
ically, refers to the one devil rather than the
individual demons: "He went about doing good and
healing all that were oppressed by the devil,
for God was with him" (Acts 10:38). Matthew contains a characteristically extensive list of the
kinds of afflictions which Jesus cured:

> And he went about all Galilee, teaching
> in their synagogues and preaching the gos-
> pel of the kingdom and healing every disease
> and every infirmity among the people. So
> his fame spread throughout all Syria, and
> they brought him all the sick, those af-
> flicted with various diseases and pains,
> demoniacs, epileptics, and paralytics, and
> he healed them. (Matthew 4:23f.)

It is well to make the point early, as such
a list makes clear, that demon possession is distinguished from physical and mental illness,
although belonging to the same general category

of disorders. As Mark 1:32 puts it, "They
brought to him all who were sick or possessed
with demons." Luke 6:17f. speaks of those "who
came to hear him and to be healed of their diseases; and those who were troubled with unclean
spirits were cured." Or again Luke says, "In
that hour he cured many of diseases and plagues
and evil spirits, and on many that were blind he
bestowed sight" (Luke 7:21). Now, as we shall
see, the demons could cause illnesses or effects
like an illness, but demon possession was considered different from illness. It was not another
way, or a primitive way, of talking about certain illnesses; nor was every case of illness
caused by demons. To be sick did not mean you
were demon afflicted, nor did demon possession
necessarily mean that you were ill.

Unclean Spirits

The conflict of Jesus with the demons began
early in his ministry. In Mark's gospel the
first event in Jesus' ministry following his baptism and calling of the disciples is the account
of the expulsion of an unclean spirit (Mark
1:21-28). Mark sets at the forefront of his narrative the account of the man with an unclean
spirit in the synagogue at Capernaum. This
account of driving out a demon is similarly the
first recorded miracle performed by Jesus in
Luke's gospel. Here is his report:

> And he went down to Capernaum, a city of
> Galilee. And he was teaching them on the
> Sabbath; and they were astonished at his

teaching, for his word was with authority.
And in the synagogue there was a man who
had the spirit of an unclean demon; and he
cried out with a loud voice, "Ah! What have
you to do with us, Jesus of Nazareth? Have
you come to destroy us? I know who you are,
the Holy One of God." But Jesus rebuked
him, saying, "Be silent, and come out of
him!" And when the demon had thrown him
down in the midst, he came out of him, having done him no harm. And they were all
amazed and said to one another, "What is
this word? For with authority and power he
commands the unclean spirits, and they come
out." And reports of him went out into
every place in the surrounding region.
(Luke 4:31-37)

In this narrative Luke uses an unusual and
somewhat clumsy expression, "spirit of an unclean
demon"; Mark says simply an "unclean spirit," the
phrase he often uses where Luke has "demon." The
terminology indicates that the demons are spiritual beings, but evil or impure spirits, not holy
spirits or good angels. It is this spiritual
nature which permits them to enter a human person. Once more we notice that the demon had his
own distinct personality. He was different from
the person in whom he dwelled and was able to
control the person he possessed to the extent of
throwing him down. The demon recognized the
distinction of personalities but associated the
possessed person with himself to the extent of
using the first person plural pronoun, "us,"
when he said, "What have you to do with us?"
(Luke 4:34)

Holy One

The demon in the Jewish synagogue at

Capernaum approached Jesus with the same question as did the demon in the Gentile region of
the Gerasenes (Luke 8:28), "What have you to do
with us [me]?" In both cases the demons had a
superhuman knowledge of Jesus' true identity
which human beings did not as yet have: in Luke
4 as "the Holy One of God" and in Luke 8 as "Son
of the Most High God." The spirit of an "impure
demon," an unholy one, stands in contrast to
Christ as the "Holy One." Perhaps the use of
these titles for Jesus was an effort by the
demon to claim power over him, but if so, the
demon was defeated in his own realm by a superior power.

The acknowledgement of Jesus is one of the
regular features of New Testament references to
demons. As spiritual beings, they knew who he
was. In Mark 3:11 we read, "And whenever the
unclean spirits beheld him, they fell down before him and cried out, 'You are the Son of God.'"
But Jesus would not accept testimony from
demons. The next verse in Mark (3:12) adds,
"And he strictly ordered them not to make him
known." Similarly in the healing of the man in
the synagogue at Capernaum, Jesus told the
demon, "Be silent, and come out of him!" (Luke
4:35; Mark 1:25). Luke 4:41 declares, "And
demons also came out of many, crying, 'You are
the Son of God!' But he rebuked them, and would
not allow them to speak, because they knew that
he was the Christ." Jesus was not ready for his

identity to be revealed, and he did not want to
be known just as a miracle worker; but another
factor in his command of silence in this case
was that he did not want to accept testimony
from such a source. He did not want the testimony of evil spirits. The apostle Paul took the
same attitude. Luke's second volume, the book
of Acts, tells the following incident when Paul,
Silas, and Luke himself were preaching in
Philippi:

> As we were going to the place of prayer,
> we were met by a slave girl who had a
> spirit of divination and brought her owners
> much gain by soothsaying. She followed
> Paul and us, crying, "These men are ser-
> vants of the Most High God, who proclaim to
> you the way of salvation." And this she
> did for many days. But Paul was annoyed,
> and turned and said to the spirit, "I
> charge you in the name of Jesus Christ to
> come out of her." And it came out that
> very hour. (Acts 16:16-18)

The association of demons with divination and
oracles in paganism will be taken up further in
the next chapter.

The demons' faith makes them an excellent
example of those who know but do not. James
2:19 cites the demons as examples of those who
have faith without works: "You believe that
God is one: you do well. Even the demons
believe--and shudder." Their faith in God and
recognition of Jesus as God's Son does not lead
to obedience; but they are excellently sit-
uated to know the facts whereof they speak. But

theirs is not a saving faith. They believe but
do not obey; they know but do not.

With a Word

The most notable feature of the expelling
of the demon from the man in the synagogue in
Capernaum to those who were present was the manner in which it was done. "What is this word?
For with authority and power he commands the unclean spirits, and they come out" (Luke 4:36).
As with the other cases where Jesus drove out a
demon, he commanded and the demon had to obey.
He accomplished the work simply by speaking an
authoritative word. Matthew 8:16 notes that "he
cast out the spirits with a word." Thus Jesus'
expulsions of the demons were not technically
exorcisms: he did not adjure them or pronounce
a formula, to which the word "exorcism" technically refers. The practice (as we know from
the magical papyri) was to say, "I adjure you,"
and invoke a superior power, often with considerable elaboration of names, and then give
the command to obey the exorcist. There were
also accompanying material means customarily employed, as the mixing of potions, offering
sacrifices, and the like. Nevertheless, the
word exorcism is used loosely and generally for
any act of driving out demons, and in keeping
with current practice of many writers I too
shall occasionally use this familiar shorthand
term for driving out demons, however performed.
In a curious twist, one of the two places in the

New Testament where the formula which exorcists
used is employed is in words of demons addressed
to Jesus. Mark quotes the Gerasene demoniac as
saying, "I adjure you by God, do not torment me"
(Mark 5:7). The demon attempted to adjure
Jesus, or exorcize him, but was unable to place
Jesus in his power. The one place where the
noun "exorcists" appears in the New Testament,
and the one other place where a formula of
adjuration appears, is in another of Luke's narratives concerning the apostle Paul, this time
in Ephesus:

> And God did extraordinary miracles by
> the hands of Paul . . . . Then some of the
> itinerant Jewish exorcists undertook to
> pronounce the name of the Lord Jesus over
> those who had evil spirits, saying, "I
> adjure you by the Jesus whom Paul preaches."
> Seven sons of a Jewish high priest named
> Sceva were doing this. But the evil spirit
> answered them, "Jesus I know, and Paul I
> know; but who are you?" And the man in
> whom the evil spirit was leaped on them,
> mastered all of them, and overpowered them,
> so that they fled out of that house naked
> and wounded. (Acts 19:11-16)

This incident reminds us that there were
Jews, and indeed others, who practiced exorcism
in the first-century world. We will have more
to say about such in this chapter and in following chapters, but we may say now that the
spiritual values emphasized by Christ and
Christians were quite different from what was
found in contemporary exorcists: instead of
expelling demons as an end in itself or for

personal gain or notoreity, they did so for
moral purposes and to emphasize the power of
God and his son, Jesus Christ, and the meaning
such had for human life. Moreover, the effectiveness and the methods were different. Not
only did Christ, and Christian healers after
him, as we shall see later, not use a formula
invoking a superior power of the same nature as
the demons, but they also avoided material means
that could be associated with magic.[11] The New
Testament and early Christian literature indicate that they used only the word of command or
prayer. In keeping with this perspective, Luke
speaks of Jesus "casting out demons" (Luke
13:32).

Women

There is another reference in Luke's gospel
to Jesus' healing those invaded by demons which
involves a case of multiple possession. Luke
8:2 refers to "some women who had been healed of
evil spirits and infirmities: Mary, called
Magdalene, from whom seven demons[12] had gone out,
and Joanna, the wife of Chuza, Herod's steward,
and Susanna, and many others." There seems to
be no sexual discrimination in demon-possession.
Women were fully equal to men in regard to the
demonic.

Deliverance

Another healing by Jesus in a synagogue,
this time on a sabbath day, and another healing
of a woman, involves a connection with the
demonic.

> Now he was teaching in one of the syna-
> gogues on the sabbath. And there was a
> woman who had had a spirit of infirmity for
> eighteen years; she was bent over and could
> not fully straighten herself. And when
> Jesus saw her, he called her and said to
> her, "Woman, you are freed from your infir-
> mity." And he laid his hands upon her, and
> immediately she was made straight, and she
> praised God. But the ruler of the syna-
> gogue, indignant because Jesus had healed
> on the sabbath, said to the people, "There
> are six days on which work ought to be done;
> come on those days and be healed, and not
> on the sabbath day. Then the Lord answered
> him, "You hypocrites! Does not each of you
> on the sabbath untie his ox or his ass from
> the manger, and lead it away to water it?
> And ought not this woman, a daughter of
> Abraham whom Satan bound for eighteen
> years, be loosed from this bond on the
> sabbath day?" (Luke 13:10-16)

The "spirit of infirmity" suggests a physical
ailment caused by a spirit; thus this is a healing miracle and not an expulsion or exorcism of
an evil spirit. The demons cause illness, but
not all illnesses were caused by them. It is
notable that verse 16 attributes the affliction
to Satan;[13] what is done by one of his spirits
is done by Satan himself. Jesus sees one unified force of evil as oppressing mankind.
According to the Pharisaic interpretations of
the law of Moses which prohibited work on the
sabbath, the practice of medicine and healing
were prohibited. Jesus, on the other hand, saw
the sabbath as an appropriate day for manifes-
ting the work of God. Since the sabbath
commemorated the deliverance of Israel from

bondage in Egypt,[14] it was appropriate on this day to deliver this woman from the oppression of Satan. Since, moreover, the Pharisees allowed an animal to be untied on the sabbath and led to water, how much more was it appropriate to un-bind a human being bound by Satan and so cause her to praise God.

Disciples

Jesus not only exercised authority over the demons himself, but he also gave the same authority to his disciples. "And he called the twelve together and gave them power and author-ity over all demons and to cure diseases, and he sent them out to preach the kingdom of God and to heal" (Luke 9:1,2). The activity of the twelve apostles (Luke 9:10) under the limited commission during Jesus' personal ministry pre-pares us for their broadening of this work under the great commission after the resurrection. So Luke tells us in Acts 5:16 that "The people also gathered from the towns around Jerusalem, bring-ing the sick and those afflicted with unclean spirits, and they were healed." And later in Acts 8:7 when Philip the evangelist, not the apostle Philip, went to Samaria, he preached and performed miracles: "For unclean spirits came out of many who were possessed, crying with a loud voice" (Acts 8:7).

By Prayer

The disciples of Jesus, however, were not always successful in curing the demon possessed.

As Jesus along with Peter, James, and John des-
cended from the mount of transfiguration, there
occurred the following incident:

> A man from the crowd cried, "Teacher, I
> beg you to look upon my son, for he is my
> only child; and behold, a spirit seizes him
> and he suddenly cries out, and will hardly
> leave him. And I begged your disciples to
> cast it out, but they could not." Jesus
> answered, "O faithless and perverse genera-
> tion, how long am I to be with you and bear
> with you? Bring your son here." While he
> was coming, the demon tore him and con-
> vulsed him. But Jesus rebuked the unclean
> spirit, and healed the boy, and gave him
> back to his father. And all were
> astonished at the majesty of God. (Luke
> 9:37-43)

Note that the "demon" of verse 42 is the same as
"spirit" of verse 39. We encounter again violent behavior, the immediate effectiveness of
Jesus' word of rebuke, and the crowd's praise
to God. The description corresponds to epilepsy
--either the demon was viewed as causing the
illness itself or a behavior like that of an
epileptic seizure. We cannot tell. Mark's
account (Mark 9:17-29) is much fuller, but only
one part of his narrative do we want to pick up
here. After the cure, the disciples asked
Jesus privately in a house why they could not
cast out the demon. Jesus replied, "This kind
cannot be driven out by anything but prayer"
(Mark 9:29).[15] That seems to say that the word
of command was insufficient, or the power of the
disciples was ineffective; only the power of God

could be invoked, through a prayer for God to act according to his will.

Name of Jesus

In contrast to this failure by the disciples, there follows shortly thereafter in the text a case of apparently successful exorcism in the name of Jesus by someone not in Jesus' inner circle of disciples. John reported to Jesus, "Master, we saw a man casting out demons in your name, and we forbade him, because he does not follow with us." But Jesus said, "Do not forbid him; for he that is not against you is for you" (Luke 9:49f.). We do not know whether this "strange exorcist" as he has been called, was a disciple of Jesus apart from the twelve who had been commissioned by Jesus, a prospective disciple in a stage of transition whom Jesus was encouraging, or a wandering free-lance practitioner who had observed the success of Jesus and his disciples on other occasions and had picked up the name of Jesus (in which case his success may have been allowed by God in order to enhance the reputation and respect for the name of Jesus). Christians employed the name of Jesus in driving out demons, as we shall learn in subsequent studies. We have already noted Paul's banishing of the spirit of divination in the girl at Philippi with the words, "I charge you in the name of Jesus Christ to come out of her" (Acts 16:18), and we recall the unsuccessful efforts of the Jewish exorcists in Ephesus to capitalize on the name of Jesus (Acts 19:13).

Obedience

Jesus on another occasion remarked on those
who would use his name in exorcism:

> Not every one who says to me, "Lord,
> Lord," shall enter the kingdom of heaven,
> but he who does the will of my Father who
> is in heaven. On that day many will say to
> me, "Lord, Lord, did we not prophesy in
> your name, and cast out demons in your
> name, and do many mighty works in your
> name?" And then will I declare to them,
> "I never knew you; depart from me, you
> evildoers." (Matthew 7:21-23)

We do not know whether these were those who
had no right to use the name of Jesus, or as
seems more likely, these were disciples who did
not combine full obedience with their other
activities in Jesus' name. It is to be noted
that Jesus does not deny their exercise of
prophecy or performance of exorcisms and other
mighty works. Rather he says that these were
not the important things. These persons had not
done these things with the right attitudes, out
of obedience to God and dependence on him.
Jesus was always effective because of his perfect submission to the will of the Father. This
was also how Jesus met the temptations of the
devil--by his complete obedience to the will of
God.[16] Humble submission to God is more important than any mighty work, according to the
teaching of Jesus.

Salvation

These passages indicate that Jesus gave

power over demons to other disciples besides the twelve. And such is confirmed by Luke's narrative about the sending out of the seventy, two by two, with a similar commission as he had given the twelve (Luke 10:1ff.). Following Jesus' instructions to them, we read:

> The seventy returned with joy, saying, "Lord, even the demons are subject to us in your name!" And he said to them, "I saw Satan fall like lightning from heaven. Behold, I have given you authority to tread upon serpents and scorpions, and over all the power of the enemy; and nothing shall hurt you. Nevertheless do not rejoice in this, that the spirits are subject to you; but rejoice that your names are written in heaven." (Luke 10:17-20)

As a further note on terminology, the "demons" of verse 17 are the "spirits" (without qualification this time) in verse 20. The demons were subject to the seventy disciples "in the name" of Jesus.[17] Jesus declared that he had given them authority over the forces of evil, represented by serpents and scorpions here.[18] Jesus refers to a vision which he had, probably to be understood as a prophetic vision. He had seen Satan fall from heaven.[19] This is probably to be taken as an anticipation of the overthrow of Satan at the crucifixion and resurrection or finally at the second coming of Jesus. The success of the disciples foreshadowed the ultimate defeat of Satan. The overcoming of demons was a sign of the fall and defeat of Satan himself. This was the cosmic significance of the conflict

of Jesus and his disciples with Satan and his
demonic spirits. The final destruction of Satan
and his hosts is certain. In Matthew's account
of the healing of the Gerasene demoniac a phrase
is added to Mark and Luke's account which brings
this out: the demoniacs cry out, "Have you come
here to torment us before the time?" (Matthew
8:29). There is a time of final destruction
determined in God's plan. Jesus in his parable
of the great judgment sends away the unmerciful
"into the eternal fire prepared for the devil
and his angels" (Matthew 25:41).

The disciples, however, were not to rejoice
in their victory over the demons. For them per-
sonally something was of even greater
significance: their names were written in
heaven. Once more, the religious or spiritual
significance is underscored as primary. Thus
Jesus warns against spiritual pride and indicates that spectacular achievements do not count
so much with God. Something is of more importance: to be enrolled among God's people and so
to be saved. This may be taken as a Lucan
parallel to Matthew's words in 7:21ff. about
obeying the will of the Father being more
significant than casting out demons in Jesus'
name.

Beelzebul

The fullest amount of teaching in the
Gospels on the demons is called forth by the
Beelzebul controversy. We read from Luke's

account as follows:

> Now he was casting out a demon that was
> dumb; when the demon had gone out, the dumb
> man spoke, and the people marveled. But
> some of them said, "He casts out demons by
> Beelzebul, the prince of demons"; while
> others, to test him, sought from him a
> sign from heaven. But he, knowing their
> thoughts, said to them, "Every kingdom
> divided against itself is laid waste, and
> house falls upon house. And if Satan also
> is divided against himself, how will his
> kingdom stand? For you say that I cast out
> demons by Beelzebul. And if I cast out
> demons by Beelzebul, by whom do your sons
> cast them out? Therefore they shall be
> your judges. But if it is by the finger of
> God that I cast out demons, then the king-
> dom of God has come upon you. When a
> strong man, fully armed, guards his own
> palace, his goods are in peace; but when
> one stronger than he assails him and over-
> comes him, he takes away his armor in which
> he trusted, and divides his spoil. (Luke
> 11:14-22)

The occasion of the controversy was Jesus healing a dumb man. The demon itself is said to be
dumb, for it was usual to attribute the infirmity caused by the demon to the demon itself.[20]
But some (Matthew specifies Pharisees--12:24),
perhaps jealous of Jesus' popularity, interpreted Jesus' powers in terms of the popular
magical notions of the day. He was in league
with a more powerful demon who enabled him to
subdue lesser demons. The prince of demons is
here named Beelzebul, who is identified with
Satan in verse 18. Beelzebul was presumably a
name in common use in Jesus' day, but it is

unattested prior to the New Testament.[21] The
accusations that Jesus was himself either demon-
possessed, out of his mind, or involved in magic
appear to have been rather common.[22] The charge
had been made against John the Baptist that he
had a demon (Luke 7:33). It appears to have
been a stock charge against anyone who acted
contrary to the usual norms of behavior.

Jesus makes four arguments in reply to the
charge that he was in league with the prince of
demons.[23] The first argument (verses 17f.) is
the logical consideration that Satan would not
be conducting civil war in his own kingdom. If
Satan is casting out his own subordinates, this
would be folly and a sign of weakness in the
kingdom of evil. Satan is defeating himself.[24]
The larger consideration represented by Jesus'
perspective[25] is the essential unity of the
kingdom of evil.[26] The demons function under a
prince or ruler and are his subordinates. Evil
may have varied manifestations, but ultimately
there is only one principle of evil. Instead of
a world dominated by many warring demons (a
pagan and polytheistic conception), Jesus saw
one kingdom of Satan. The Jewish exorcists
might deal with local manifestations of demonic
activity, but Jesus saw his work as demon-
strating that the whole dominion of evil was
being conquered. The demons functioned as part
of a larger whole, the dominion of the devil.

Jesus' second argument in response to the

charge that he was in alliance with Beelzebul
was an _ad_ _hominem_ consideration. There were
Jewish exorcists going about casting out demons,
or at least claiming to do so. "Sons of" means
disciples of, and so refers to followers of his
critics. By whose power were they working, or
claiming to work? Logically the critics would
have to make the same admission about their own
wonder-workers, or if these exorcists were working by the power of God, then so was Jesus.

And that leads to the third consideration
urged by Jesus. If it was indeed only by the
power of God that demons could be cast out, then
the kingdom or rule of God was being manifested.
The phrase "finger of God" is an allusion to
Exodus 8:19 where the miracles of Moses in connection with the Exodus were attributed to the
finger of God in contrast to the wonders of the
Egyptian magicians which were worked by magic.
Jesus was accomplishing a new deliverance, by
the same power which worked through Moses.
Matthew's account (12:28) uses the phrase
"Spirit of God"; the two phrases are equivalent
in meaning, and Matthew may be understood as
interpreting the phrase used by Luke. Jesus'
defeat of the demons by the power of God was
proof that the kingdom, which means the rule or
power, of God was present in him and his ministry. That was also a demonstration that the
full establishment of the kingdom and the complete overthrow of Satan's rule was to be

effected. Jesus would presumably not allow the
same significance, at least in its fullness, to
the activity of the Jewish exorcists. This was
a debating situation and not a matter of absolute truth and consistency, but even in a
limited sphere any success by the Jews in the
name of God in driving out demons was a sign of
the power of God's kingdom and a defeat for the
kingdom of Satan. But the person of Jesus himself gave his works a greater significance than
comparable works by others.

The One Stronger

The person of Jesus and why he was able to
do his mighty works may be the clue for understanding the fourth part of Jesus' response to
his critics. The parable of the strong man may
be seen as a striking affirmation of Jesus'
power and a very meaningful illustration of the
significance of Jesus' ministry in general and
his exorcisms in particular. Luke's version of
the parable employs the imagery of warfare and a
military campaign against a fortified stronghold; Matthew (12:29) and Mark (3:27) employ the
imagery of robbery. The teaching is the same in
both cases. Satan is the strong man, dwelling
in a fortified palace. We may think of this
world as enemy-occupied territory; Satan as its
ruler has a fortress to protect his ill-gotten
possessions. But there comes one stronger than
he. The conqueror liberates the fortress, takes
away Satan's power, and takes over his

possessions for his own use. Christ as the "one stronger" than the strong man has invaded Satan's stronghold, driven away his guards (the demons), and liberated humanity in bondage to him. Not only the demons, but Satan himself, have no power in the presence of Jesus.

Verse 23, "He who is not with me is against me, and he who does not gather with me scatters," emphasizes that there can be no neutrality in the conflict between Christ and Satan.[27]

Holy Spirit

Luke places next to the account of the Beelzebul controversy another teaching of Jesus relative to unclean spirits which serves to emphasize Jesus' priorities and the spiritual values which are uppermost.

> When the unclean spirit has gone out of a man, he passes through waterless places seeking rest; and finding none he says, "I will return to my house from which I came." And when he comes he finds it swept and put in order. Then he goes and brings seven other spirits more evil than himself, and they enter and dwell there; and the last state of that man becomes worse than the first. (Luke 11:24-26)

This is a warning that exorcism by itself may do more harm than good. Something is much more significant than a mighty work in driving out demons, and for a person delivered from demons something is more important than their departure.

The reference to "waterless places" brings

us back to another item of popular belief. It
seems to be widely held, across centuries and
cultures, although not universally, that ghosts
and the like cannot cross a body of water.
Washington Irving's "Legend of Sleepy Hollow"
speaks as follows:

> The dominant spirit, however, that
> haunts this enchanted region, and seems to
> be commander-in-chief of all the powers of
> the air, is the apparition of a figure on
> horseback without a head. It is said by
> some to be the ghost of a Hessian trooper,
> whose head had been carried away by a
> cannon-ball . . . during the revolutionary
> war. . . .
>   [Brom Bones] affirmed that, on return-
> ing one night from the neighboring village
> . . . he had been overtaken by this mid-
> night trooper; that he had offered to race
> with him for a bowl of punch, and should
> have won it too, for [his horse] beat the
> goblin horse all hollow, but, just as they
> came to the church bridge [across a brook],
> the Hessian bolted, and vanished in a flash
> of fire. . . .

Ichabod Crane then had a fearful encounter with
the headless horseman as he rode home about mid-
night. His old horse could not outrun the
ghostly apparition.

> An opening in the trees now cheered him
> with the hopes that the church bridge was
> at hand. The wavering reflection of a sil-
> ver star in the bosom of the brook told him
> that he was not mistaken. . . . He recol-
> lected the place where Brom Bones's ghostly
> competitor had disappeared. "If I can but
> reach that bridge," thought Ichabod, "I am
> safe."

Of course, the story has a strange turn, as you

know. This belief about ghosts not crossing water may have something to do with the early church's doctrine about baptism freeing one from the power of demons.[28]

It was noted earlier that the demons were thought to inhabit deserted regions. Students from other parts of the country who come to West Texas for school think there is something to this about demons preferring dry wasteland and think Abilene has plenty of its share of demons. But my reply is that in some Jewish thought the demons preferred water, especially stagnant water, and the reason the demon could not find rest was that the region was waterless; so it is those influenced by demons who move on elsewhere. Be that as it may, Jesus was not concerned with items of popular belief. The notice of "waterless places" is incidental to the moral and spiritual lesson Jesus wanted to teach.

The demon of Jesus' story returned to the person from whom he had departed. Nature abhors a vacuum; the spiritual world does too. Since there was nothing that had filled up the vacancy left by the departure of the demon, he reoccupied the house, the human heart, from which he had gone out.[29] Not only that, but he brought seven other spirits more evil than himself, expressive of the more complete and intense surrender to evil.[30] There is certainly no idea here of eternal security, or once saved always saved.

The text does not expressly make an
application, but I think one is readily at hand.
Not only must evil be banished from one's life,
but it must also be filled with good. We all
know how futile it is to try to resist temptation by a simple exercise of will power. The
more we say we will not do something, the more
we think about it, and the stronger the urge
becomes. We have to get our minds on something
else altogether and think good thoughts. We
must become too busy doing something else for
the temptation to gain hold. Furthermore, we
recognize the truth of the saying, "Idleness is
the devil's workshop." Human beings are going
to be doing something. The best way to be sure
that that activity is not bad is to be busy in
doing the good. Such would be some of the psychological corollaries of what Jesus says here.
But I would suggest that there is a yet more
significant spiritual and doctrinal conclusion.

God's own alternative is to be found in the
last verse of the teaching which preceded the
Beelzebul controversy in this same eleventh
chapter of Luke: "the heavenly Father will give
the Holy Spirit to those who ask him!" (Luke
11:13). The Christian doctrine of the Holy
Spirit is important in relation to the activity
of demons. Missionaries tell me how important
the biblical teaching on the indwelling of the
Holy Spirit is to them in societies which believe in spirits and demon-possession. God's

gift of the Holy Spirit banishes unclean spirits and gives the power of a new life and new purpose to the obedient believer.[31]

Conclusions

We may now pull together some conclusions which emerge from the Gospel accounts of Jesus' encounters with the demons.

(1) Jesus accepted the demons as real, and there is no indication that he was accommodating popular superstitions. The phenomena associated with demons were as real as the sicknesses which Jesus cured or the physical infirmities which he healed, or as the human religious and political authorities which opposed him.

(2) The demons were spirit beings with superhuman strength and knowledge.

(3) But the demons are presented as impure and evil spirits, that is as spiritual beings in rebellion against God.

(4) Human beings were the scene of the struggle between Jesus and the demons. The demons could invade and gain possession of a person. The possession was not treated as a moral disorder but as in the same category as illnesses; the demon took the place of human personality. But Jesus did not consider the demons as having any rightful possession of human beings.

(5) The demons were acting under the direction of Satan and as part of his kingdom. Thus Jesus viewed his enemy as a unified kingdom

of evil: he was fighting the same hostile power
when overcoming temptation, delivering the
possessed, and healing the sick.[32]

(6) Jesus has authority over demons. The
exorcisms performed by Jesus, if we may use this
shorthand, or the casting out of demons, if one
prefers that manner of speaking, were a victo-
rious combat with the devil and his kingdom.
They were a sign of the nearness of the kingdom
and a preparation for its coming in fullness.
The subjection of the demons was not yet the
real thing, that is the final victory over evil,
but it was an effective anticipation of the
eschatological events.

(7) The final overthrow and destruction of
the devil and his angels is certain, because of
the authority exercised by Christ over them.
There is no doubt about the final outcome.

(8) Jesus gave his disciples authority over
the demons. Where the name of Jesus is confess-
ed, they have no power and there is nothing to
fear from them. Where there is the Holy Spirit,
there is no place for evil spirits.

(9) That which gave Jesus his authority
over the demons was his perfect obedience to the
will of the Father. And that is what permits
his disciples to share in his victory, being
humbly and submissively obedient to God.

(10) There are religious and spiritual
values of much greater importance than the de-
mons--i.e. one's own relationship to God and
Christ.

[1]Matthew's account, in 8:31, contains the
only use of daimōn (in the plural) in the New
Testament; all other passages use daimonion, but
there seems no difference in meaning; and I am
using the words interchangeably. Mark's account
(5:1-20) uses "unclean spirit," as he commonly
does, in place of "demon"; this difference in
terminology is again without difference in
meaning.

[2]Cf. 4 Maccabees 18:8, "seducer of the
desert"; 1 Enoch 10:4f.; Luke 11:21.

[3]bSanhedrin 65b, quoted in Chapter III.

[4]bErubin 41b, "Three things deprive a man
of his senses and of a knowledge of his creator,
viz., idolators, an evil spirit, and oppressive
poverty." Cf. Philostratus, Life of Apollonius
IV.20 for a parallel to the demon possessions
of the Gospels. Juan B. Cortés, S.J. and
Florence M. Gatti, The Case against Possession
and Exorcisms (New York: Vantage Press, 1975)
in their reaction against modern sensational
stories argue that there never were demons, only
the devil and his angels, and so the exorcisms
of the Gospels were not actually casting out of
demons but cures of "internal" diseases and
daimonizomai should not be translated "possessed
by demons" but "afflicted by evil or malignant
powers or forces." Although modern sensation-
alism may read unfortunate ideas into the text,
I have retained the conventional translation
"possessed by," while understanding it in the
sense of "afflicted by." Modern perspectives
should not lead to a denial that the Biblical
text reflected the beliefs of its time about
demons.

[5]Philostratus, ibid.

[6]Cf. the magical papyri, as Paris Mag. Pap.
3007-3085, quoted in C. K. Barrett, The New
Testament Background (New York: Macmillan,
1957), pp. 31-33.

[7]Josephus, _Antiquities_ VIII.47f.

[8]Philostratus, _Life of Apollonius_ IV.10.

[9]1 Enoch 21; cf. Revelation 20:1-3.

[10]For a similar study based on the demon narratives in Mark see J. Ramsey Michaels, "Jesus and the Unclean Spirits," _Demon Possession_, ed. J. W. Montgomery (Minneapolis: Bethany Fellowship, 1976), pp. 41-57.

[11]W. Foerster, "Daimōn, daimonion," _Theological Dictionary of the New Testament_, ed. G. Kittel, Vol. II (Grand Rapids: Eerdmans Publishing Co., 1964), p. 19. That the distinctions were not absolute but depended on what one considered a magical formula and magical material has been rightly shown by Harold Remus, _Pagan-Christian Conflict over Miracle in the Second Century_ (Cambridge: Philadelphia Patristic Foundation, 1983), especially pp. 48-72. A more one-sided interpretation of the evidence which placed Jesus in the category of the wonder-workers and magicians of his time is Morton Smith, _Jesus the Magician_ (San Francisco: Harper and Row, 1978). See also Campbell Bonner, "Traces of Thaumaturgic Technique in the Miracles," _Harvard Theological Review_ 20(1927), pp. 171-181; and idem, "The Technique of Exorcism," _Harvard Theological Review_ 36(1943), pp. 39-49.

[12]Cf. Luke 11:26. _Testament of Reuben_ 2:11 speaks of "seven spirits of deceit."

[13]For indications of sickness as a work of Satan cf. Acts 10:38 and perhaps 2 Corinthians 12:7.

[14]Deuteronomy 5:15.

[15]Some witnesses to the text add "fasting," which was an accompaniment to prayer on serious occasions in the life of the early church, so

this reading may reflect early Christian practice. Matthew 17:20 attributes the disciples'
failure to little faith.

[16]Luke 4:1-13; Matthew 4:1-11.

[17]Cf. Mark 16:17.

[18]Cf. Genesis 3:15; Deuteronomy 8:15;
Isaiah 11:8; Mark 16:17f.

[19]Cf. Revelation 12:7-12.

[20]Cf. Mark 9:25.

[21]Beelzebul is usually derived from
Baalzebub (2 Kings 1:2). This word was a Hebrew
pun ("lord of the flies") on the name of a
Philistine or Canaanite god. Beelzebul is
apparently the same as Belial (Beliar), met in
the intertestamental Jewish literature--see
chapter III and cf. 2 Corinthians 6:15.

[22]For the charge that Jesus had a demon, see
John 7:20; 8:48-52; that he was mad, see John
10:20f.; Mark 3:21; the present episode implies
the use of magic, and the charge was made
explicit later--cf. Origen, Against Celsus I.6
and references in note 11.

[23]Cf. Eusebius, Treatise Against Life of
Apollonius by Philostratus 26, "For Apollonius,
as they say, drives out one demon with the help
of another." The idea was common in magic.

[24]No consideration is given to the possibility that Satan was acting in pretence in order
to perpetrate a greater deception by getting the
people to follow an imposter. Exactly this consideration was urged by some Christian
apologists later against the wonders and cures
performed by pagans: i.e. the demons enabled
magicians and charlatans to do certain things
in order to deceive the people. E.g. Origen,
Against Celsus II.49-51.

[25]And this obviates the objection considered in the preceding note.

[26]Trevor Ling, The Significance of Satan: New Testament Demonology and its Contemporary Relevance (London: SPCK, 1961) particularly urges this consideration.

[27]2 Corinthians 6:14-16.

[28]See chapter IV.

[29]Josephus, Antiquities VIII.45, Solomon "left behind forms of exorcisms with which those possessed by demons drive them out never to return"; 47, Eleazar, "adjured the demon never to come back into" a cured man. That demons require a home, see Aelian, Characteristics of Animals XI.32.

[30]Cf. 2 Peter 2:20-22 for the last state becoming worse than the first.

[31]Romans 8 and Galatians 5; see further chapter V.

[32]Ragnar Levistad, Christ the Conqueror (New York: Macmillan, 1954), Section III.B.

CHAPTER II

GREEK VIEWS ON DEMONOLOGY

What was the historical background to the
views about demons expressed in the Gospels?
The two principal contributions to this immediate background were made by the Greeks and the
Jews. We begin this background study with a
history of Greek thought about demons.

The life of Plutarch (c. A. D. 50 to 120)
overlaps that of the apostles, and his writings
were produced not long after most of the New
Testament books. The opinions expressed in
Plutarch's wide range of writings cover most of
the views expressed by Greeks on the subject of
demons.[1] One passage in particular provides a
convenient summary and starting point for
discussion.

> Those persons have resolved more and
> greater complexities who have set the race
> of demons midway between gods and men. . . .
> Among the Greeks, Homer appears to use both
> names [gods and demons] in common and some-
> times to speak of the gods as demons.
> Hesiod was the first to set forth clearly
> and distinctly four classes of rational
> beings: gods, demons, heroes, in this
> order, and last of all, men. . . .
>
> Others postulate a transmutation . . . .
> The better souls obtain their transmutation
> from men into heroes and from heroes into
> demons. But from the demons a few souls
> still, in the long reach of time, because
> of supreme excellence, come, after being
> purified, to share completely in divine
> qualities. But with some of these souls it
> comes to pass that they do not maintain
> control over themselves, but yield to

temptation and are again clothed with mortal bodies and have a dim and darkened
life, like mist or vapor.

. . . .

The clear testimony from ancient times
[is] that in the intermediate regions between the gods and men there exist certain
natures susceptible to human emotions and
involuntary changes, whom it is right that
we, like our fathers before us, should
regard as demons, and, calling them by that
name, should reverence them.

Xenocrates, the companion of Plato,
[speaks] of the nature of demons as having
human emotions but godlike power. . . .

Let us not listen to any who say that
there are some oracles not divinely inspired by the gods; and on the other hand
let us not imagine that the god goes in and
out and is present at these ceremonies and
helps in conducting them; but let us commit
these matters to those ministers of the
gods to whom it is right to commit them, as
to servants and clerks, and let us believe
that demons are guardians of sacred rites
of the gods and prompters in the mysteries,
while others go about as avengers of arro-
gant and grievous cases of injustice. . . .
As among men, so also among the demons,
there are different degrees of excellence,
and in some there is a weak and dim remainder of the emotional and irrational, a
survival, as it were, while in others this
is excessive and hard to stifle.

As for festivals and sacrifices, which
may be compared with ill-omened and gloomy
days, in which occur the eating of raw
flesh, rending of victims, fasting, and
beating of breasts, and again in many
places scurrilous language at the shrines
. . . I should say that these acts are not
performed for any god, but are soothing and
appeasing rites for the averting of evil

demons. Nor is it credible that the gods
demanded or welcomed the human sacrifices
of ancient days. . . .

As for the various tales of rapine and
wanderings of the gods, their concealments
and banishment and servitude, which men re-
hearse in myths and songs, all these are,
in fact, not things that were done to the
gods or happened to them, but to the demons
. . . . With the departure of the demons
assigned to the oracles and prophetic
shrines occurs the decline of the oracles
themselves.[2]

This passage includes the following meanings of the word demon: (1) equivalent to a god
or that which is divine; (2) the souls of the
deceased with the capacity for change into other
levels of being; and (3) intermediary spiritual
beings which may become either good or bad. Not
developed in this passage but attested elsewhere
in Plutarch is another meaning: (4) a personal
guardian spirit. Our purpose in this chapter
will be to illustrate these meanings and their
various ramifications in Greek literature. We
will explore their interrelationships , and then
show how these Greek concepts were part of the
common background of popular belief in early
Christian times. We should not infer from
Plutarch that there was a straight line of
development in Greek thinking, nor form the impression of a perfectly logical system of
thought about demons. The linguistic usage was
often fluid, and what we find is a collection of
ideas, often overlapping and not completely

consistent with one another. But these ideas
and word usages are rooted in common human experiences and had great influence on the future,
even in the history of Christianity.

Expanding on the four meanings in Plutarch,
we will discuss the word usage about demons
under seven headings employing an alliteration
on the letter D (for demons): (1) the divine
(gods), (2) destiny (as divinely sent or appointed), (3) the deceased (departed souls), (4)
defending (guardian) spirits, (5) divine intermediaries, (6) the demonic, and (7) demon
possession. We start with the first usage of
the word demon to which Plutarch refers, as
equivalent to the gods.[3]

The Divine

The word demon in classical Greek meant a
divine or superhuman power or activity. It
possessed for the ancient Greeks none of the
negative or evil associations which it has for
us. As Plutarch says, Homer used the word in
reference to the deities, and sometimes interchangeably with the word "god" (theos). Thus we
read that Athena went to Olympus, home of Zeus,
"with the other demons."[4] In another place where
someone rushed upon another "like a demon," he
was told by Apollo, "Do not wish to be like the
gods."[5] This usage persisted. Isocrates in the
fourth century B. C. gives this advice: "First
of all show devotion to the gods. . . . Do honor
always to the demonic" (i.e. the divine, the

gods in general).[6] Dio Cassius in the third
century A. D. reports the emperor Augustus under
whom Jesus was born as saying in a speech, "Who
is found more divine [demonic] than I?"[7]

One of the protective spirits of the house-
hold in Greece was known as the Agathos Daimōn,
the "Good Demon" or spirit. It was visualized
as a house snake. At the close of a meal a
libation was poured out to the Agathos Daimōn,
and at dinner parties a libation was drunk to
it.[8]

As some of the above examples indicate,
"demon" was used more commonly when the identity
of a specific god was unknown or when the emphasis was more on the power or activity of the
deity rather than on the personality or identity.
The word in these instances is better translated
"heaven" or "divine power." Thus in Homer we
read, "When a man wants to fight contrary to the
divine power [daimona] with another whom a god
honors, immediately great woe overwhelms him."[9]
The word in this impersonal sense often occurs
in reference to what is divine in contrast to
what is human. Herodotus reports the different
interpretations of a defeat in battle suffered
by the Athenians: "The Argives say it was they,
and the Athenians that it was a divine power
[daimonion] that destroyed the Attic army."[10]
The orator Aeschines refers to a "folly not of
men but heaven-sent [daimonios]"[11] Plato declares that the divine [daimonion] "is

absolutely incapable of falsehood."[12] This use
for an indefinite deity or divine power also
persisted into the early Christian age, as may
be seen from Dio Chrysostom around 100 in his
question, "What divine power [daimonion] must
one propitiate?" and in his reference to an
altar erected at a spot in the belief "that some
deity [daimonion] was there."[13]

   A very common use of demon in the sense of
impersonal divine power is to refer to something
as "heaven-sent," when one did not know what
caused it or to what deity to refer it. That
master of tragedy Sophocles refers to a "work of
heaven."[14] What is heaven-sent may be good--
"heaven-blessed,"[15] a "marvellous divine gift";[16]
or it may be bad--"heaven-sent woes,"[17] "demonized by evils."[18] This usage includes what was
marvellous or wondrous[19] or only a strange co-
incidence.[20] The idea of simply a superhuman
power, but not specifically or necessarily
divine, is present in Aristotle's explanation
that dreams have a divine origin [daimonia] but
are not God-sent, "for nature is divinely or-
dained [daimonia] but not itself divine
[theia]."[21]

Destiny

   The word demonic as meaning marvellous or
heaven-sent shaded off into the meaning of fortune, luck, or chance. This meaning was very
common. It may be seen as a permutation from
the meaning of "the divine." Thus something

could be spoken of as happening "by the luck of
heaven" (tycha daimonos)[22] or "by chance."[23]
Since "whatsoever from heaven [daimonion]is sent
hath sovereign sway,"[24] there is often the idea
of what is predetermined, that is fate or destiny. The poet Bacchlides refers to a "destiny
not to be resisted" (amachos daimōn) and again
to "what the demons [daimones] will."[25] "Each
one has his own fate appointed" (daimonizomai).26
Sometimes it is difficult to know whether the
idea is more fortune (chance) or destiny (fate),
and it may not have been clear in the author's
mind. Pausanias in the second century of the
Christian era reflected on how heaven (to
daimonion) is always willing something new, and
all things are being changed by chance (tychē).[27]

   Without the idea of destiny, the word could
refer simply to one's lot in life, so Hesiod
says, "Whatever be your lot [daimoni], work is
best for you."[28] The idea of destiny or fate
could pertain specifically to one's final outcome. "I will deal you fate [a demon, daimona]"
meant, "I will kill you."[29]

   This usage of demon as referring to the
power controlling the destiny of individuals or
groups also goes back to Homer. Odysseus lamen-
ted, "An evil doom of some god [daimonos] was my
undoing, and measureless wine."[30] We may feel
that the wine had more to do with it, and like
many today Odysseus was blaming on bad luck what
was more due to too much liquor! One passage in

Homer reflects the future linguistic development
in assigning affliction to a demon and healing
to the gods: "A father who lies in sickness,
bearing cruel pains . . . and some demon assails
him, . . .but the gods [theoi] free him."[31]

One's destiny, of course, could be good.
And Plato, who fairly consistently uses demon in
a good sense, refers to the "demon of good fortune" (daimonia tychē).[32] But it seems far more
common to refer to the destiny spirit as bringing bad luck. Oedipus blamed his circumstances
on some "inhuman power" (daimonos).[33] A line in
Aeschylus reads, "Some destructive power or evil
demon [kakos daimōn] caused the beginning of our
utter rout."[34]

A power dispensing one's fortune or fate
could easily be personalized as a spirit. Before following up this line of development, some
other views which gave personal identity to the
demons must be traced.

The Deceased

Plutarch, as we read at the beginning,
referred to Hesiod, who lived about 700 B. C.,
as the first to set forth four classes of
rational beings. Hesiod taught that the gods
created a golden race of men who lived without
toil and grief. When they died and were buried,
"they are called pure demons [daimones] dwelling
on the earth, and are kindly, delivering from
harm, guardians of mortal men; for they roam
everywhere over the earth, clothed in mist, and

keep watch on judgments and cruel deeds."[35] As
a Platonist Plutarch may have derived his respect for Hesiod's views from Plato. Plato also
referred to Hesiod's view, and apparently on the
basis of it suggested that good men became
demons on death.[36] Hesiod, therefore, appears
to be the source for the idea that demons and
heroes are the souls of the deceased who had
been divinized, but Plato to be the source of
the idea developed in Plutarch that souls can
rise to the status of heroes, then demons, and
finally the gods, or may fall back and be
clothed with mortal bodies.[37]

That demons were the souls of the deceased
was actually a fairly common Greek idea. Hesiod
in another passage said that Aphrodite caught up
a young boy and made him a keeper of her shrine
by night, "a demon" [daimona].[38] Euripides in a
reference to a deceased woman says, "a blessed
demon she is now."[39] The association of the
demons with the gods of the underworld derives
from this identification of demons with the
souls of the deceased.[40]

Authors in the second century of the
Christian era made frequent mention of demons
as souls of the departed.[41] Lucian of Samosata
wrote a satire about a Cynic named Proteus who
as an act of self-glorification staged a suicide
by casting himself into a bonfire. Proteus expressed the view that he was going to become a
guardian spirit (demon) of the night.[42] Then at

the time of the self-immolation he said, "Demons
of my mother and father, receive me with favor."[43]
Pausanias related the story of a demon (or
ghost) of a man who had been stoned to death
attacking and killing others.[44] This idea of
the soul of a person violently put to death ter-
rorizing others has remained a part of popular
folklore under the terminology of ghosts instead
of demons.[45]

Defending Spirits

Pausanias could be referring not to a dis-
embodied soul but to the individual guardian
spirit which accompanies each person. Such is
another common usage of the term demon in Greek
literature. I think Pausanias has "ghost" in
mind, but the reason for uncertainty is that
Plutarch tells a story of a similar kind where
it is clearly a guardian spirit involved. "The
great guardian spirit [daimōn] of Caesar, whose
help he had enjoyed through life, followed upon
him even after death as an avenger of his mur-
der."[46] Plutarch continues with an account of
the visions in which the demon of Caesar appeared to Brutus to frighten him.

Since the soul seemed somehow inexplicable
or even "superhuman" and could be conceived as
separate from body life, it was possible for the
concept of soul to be united with the idea of an
individual destiny or fate to produce the concept of a personal destiny spirit. It is difficult, however, to be sure of the line of

development or to determine which view influenced the other.[47] The passage quoted at the beginning does not include the concept of an individual guardian spirit in its survey of opinions, but Plutarch elsewhere shows a knowledge of the view and it was firmly rooted in the Platonic tradition.

Socrates appears to have been the point of departure for this philosophical development.[48] He often talked of his _daimonion_, which he heard as a kind of negative voice restraining him from certain actions; when it said nothing he felt it was all right to proceed with a planned action.[49] Socrates seems to be describing something like the conscience, except that his inner voice had a premonitory function as well as passing judgment on past actions.[50]

Plato then elaborated the idea of each person having his own guardian spirit. Each one chooses his own demon: "No demon shall cast lots for you, but you shall choose your own deity."[51] The idea is related to that of destiny later in the passage: "Lachesis sent with each, as the guardian of his life and the fulfiller of his choice, the demon that he had chosen, and this demon led the soul first to Clotho, under her hand and her turning of the spindle to ratify the fate of his lot and choice."[52] In another context Plato describes a conflict going on among us: "Gods and demons [are] our allies, and we are their property . . .

but upon this earth there dwell souls possessing
an unjust spirit."[53]   After death the demon of
each one, to whom he belonged in life, leads him
to the place where the dead are gathered, and
after judgment they pass into the world below.[54]
Plutarch adds the point that the demons as
guardian spirits do not assist all indifferently
but those who have striven and are nearing
success.[55] In other words this is divine assist-
ance to those who prove themselves worthy and
not an expression of divine favoritism.

The Stoic philosophers picked up this idea
of the guardian spirit and made the demons
general supervisory spirits. Diogenes Laertius
reports concerning the older Stoa that they
"hold that there are demons who are in sympathy
with mankind and watch over human affairs."[56]
The later Stoic philosophers of the first
Christian centuries integrated this idea into
their pantheistic view in which the rational
soul in man was a part of the divine rational
principle of all reality. Epictetus puts the
view this way:

> Zeus has stationed (by each man's side) as
> guardian his demon and has committed the
> man to his care and that too a guardian
> who never sleeps and is not to be beguiled.
> For to what other guardian, better and
> more careful, could he have committed each
> one of us?

He continues by claiming that you should never
say that you are alone: "God is within and your
own demon is within."[57] Marcus Aurelius is even

more explicit:

> And he lives with the gods who con-
> stantly shows them that his soul is
> satisfied with what is assigned to him,
> and that it obeys all the divinity wills--
> that divinity which Zeus has given every
> man as his guardian and guide, a portion
> of himself, his understanding and reason.[58]

Elsewhere Epictetus seems to approximate the
demon within to the conscience: "Think the matter over more carefully, know yourself, ask the
demon, do not attempt the task without God."[59]

Divine Intermediaries

These views of a personal destiny spirit,
an individual guardian spirit, and of a voice
within were obviously very significant for later
ideas of fate, guardian angels, and the conscience; but as far as the terminology of demons
is concerned, another idea developed by Plato
was much more significant. In a passage funda-
mental to the whole future development of
thought about demons, Plato sets forth the position of demons as lesser divine beings,
intermediaries between the gods and humans.
This particular development of Hesiod's classification of rational beings was important to
Plutarch's demonology and is illuminating to the
Christian use of the word demon. The passage
occurs in Plato's Symposium:

> For the whole of the demonic is between
> the divine and the mortal." "Possessing
> what power?" I asked. "Interpreting and
> conveying human things to the gods and
> divine things to men; prayers and sacri-
> fices from below, and ordinances and

punishments from above. Being midway between, it makes each to supplement the
other, so that the whole is combined in
one. Through it are conveyed all divina-
tions, and all soothsaying and sorcery.
God with man does not mingle: but the
demonic is the means of all association
and converse of men with gods and of gods
with men, whether waking or asleep."
[202E-203A]

Plato may have drawn this idea from Pythagoras,
but the source which attributes a similar view
to him may have been describing the Neo-
pythagoreans who were active at the beginning of
the Christian era. The passage in question
attributed the following belief to Pythagoras:

The whole air is full of souls which are
called demons or heroes; these are they who
send men dreams and signs of future disease
and health . . . and it is to them that
purifications, lustrations, all divination,
omens, and the like have reference.[60]

Plato also has Socrates suggest that the demons
are a kind of gods or children of gods by nymphs
or others.[61] They assisted in the creation of
the world.[62] Another extended passage, the
authorship of which is disputed but certainly
coming from Plato's school, further elaborates
on the intermediary position and function of
demons. After mentioning the traditional
Olympic gods and the visible gods (the greatest
of whom are the stars) the author places next
the demons, an

air-borne race, holding the third and
middle space, the source of interpretation,
whom we must specially honor with prayers

> for the sake of an auspicious journey
> across [from earth to heaven after death]
> . . . . They understand the whole of our
> thoughts and show extraordinary kindness to
> anyone of us who is a good and true man,
> and hate him who is utterly evil. . . . The
> heaven being full of live creatures, they
> interpret all men and all things both to
> one another and to the most exalted gods,
> because the middle creatures move both to
> earth and to the whole of heaven with a
> lightly rushing motion.[63]

This view of demons as "mid-way between gods and men, conveying above prayers and petitions of men and bringing below the oracles and gifts of good things"[64] was developed in the Platonic school, as the passage from Plutarch at the beginning indicates, in such a way as to make the demons themselves the real recipients of religious ceremonies, particularly those of a grosser nature which philosophical thought came to regard as unworthy of the divine.[65] Plutarch further witnesses to the way in which demons (as intermediaries) could be brought in to explain aspects of the functioning and of the decline of the oracles.[66]

Plato understood the gods as being assisted by the demons. He referred to the "gods and their attendant demons."[67] Later Plutarch could refer to demons called by the names of the gods with whom they were allied.[68] This view made it easy to attribute to the attendant demon things ascribed to the deity which might seem unworthy or philosophically difficult to accept. Plato himself viewed the demons predominantly as beneficent beings. They were beneficent ruling powers in the golden age,[69] and different parts of the universe had been distributed under them.[70] Plato's student Xenocrates, however, correlated their intermediate position with a mixed nature, combining human emotions and divine power. On the analogy of human souls, which may be either good or bad, the demons could exert their influence for either good or bad.[71]

Xenocrates systematized demonology along the lines of Plato's classification of beings. Plutarch is the principal source of that systematization, in the passage quoted at the beginning and in the following passage:

> Plato, Pythagoras, Xenocrates, and Chrysippus, following the lead of early writers on sacred subjects, allege the demons to have been stronger than men and in their might greatly surpassing our nature, yet not possessing the divine quality unmixed and uncontaminated, but with a share also in the nature of the soul and in the perceptive faculties of the body and with a susceptibility to pleasure and pain and to whatsoever other experience is incident to these mutations and is the source of much disquiet in some and of less in others. For in demons, as in men, there are divers degrees of virtue and of vice.[72]

Demons, on this view, might move either up or down.[73] Plutarch explained that the Egyptian gods Isis and Osiris changed from demons into gods, whereas Typhon as a "demonic power" became bad.[74]

The Demonic

The natural tendency was increasingly to attribute bad things to these intermediary beings. The demons provided a convenient explanation to account for many things: the disasters and evils in the world (imperfections not to be blamed on the supreme gods), superstitious religious practices (unworthy of pure deities), the immoralities of the gods in mythology (really told about demons not the unchangeable gods).

Since the demons were of a "complex and inconsistent nature," Xenocrates referred many features of the popular religion to them:

> Such days as are days of ill omen, and such festivals as have associated with them either beatings or lamentations or fastings or scurrilous language or ribald jests have no relation to the honors paid to the gods or to worthy demons, but he [Xenocrates] believes that there exist in the space about us certain great and powerful natures, obdurate, however, and morose, which take pleasure in such things as these, and if they succeed in obtaining them, resort to nothing worse.[75]

Apuleius of Madaura in the second century A. D. shows how Plato's thought was extended in a sinister direction:

> I believe Plato when he asserts that there are certain divine powers holding a position and possessing a character midway between gods and men, and that all divination and the miracles of magicians are controlled by them.[76]

The literature around New Testament times
has more to say about malevolent demons than
about good demons. Plutarch in his <u>Lives</u> relates how both Dion and Brutus were given an
intimation by a demon of their approaching death.
He comments then on those who say no man in his
right mind was ever visited by an apparition of
a demon or a spectre; who say little children,
foolish women, and men deranged by sickness have
indulged in empty and strange imaginings because
they had an evil demon of superstition in themselves. The religiously conservative, although
rationalistic, Plutarch, without accepting all
the popular tales, nevertheless replies that men
should accept the doctrine of olden times that
mean and malignant demons do make appearances to
confound and terrify good men out of envy.[77] He
repeats a saying which shows the trend of his
thought: "What is most helpful? God. What is
most harmful? Demon."[78]

The popular Stoic philosophy accepted the
common terminology and outlook on demons.
Chrysippus suggested that evil demons were in
charge of some aspects of life.[79] Later Stoics
thought "that evil demons stalk about, whom the
gods use as executioners and avengers upon unholy and unjust men."[80] The execution of
punishment was generally regarded as a task of
the demons, not of the high gods or Olympians.[81]

The Hermetic literature of the second and
third centuries A. D. shows a blending of

Platonic and Stoic thought in its references to
demons as in other things. Thus the tasks assigned to demons were to watch over the affairs
of men, work disasters, and give retribution.[82]
Demons are everywhere in the world; and the evil
demons are the cause of evil in the world.[83]
They are the divine beings who live nearest to
men.[84] The demons are innumerable, and souls
after death must pass through their numbers in
order to reach God.[85] There is an avenging
demon who kindles the fire for the unrighteous.[86]

We have thus reached elements of Greek
thought which clearly are in the background of
New Testament times and influenced Christian
thinking in the post-biblical times. There is
one further aspect of this background especially
relevant for understanding the New Testament and
the situation in the early church. This has to
do with the belief that demons could take possession of a human being and with the efforts
made to expel such demons.

Demon Possession

To understand Greek ideas of demon possession we must take note of one further usage of
the word "demon," that with reference to a person who was mad or insane. This usage may be
introduced by a passage which makes a play on
the two meanings of the word "demon" as referring to something supernatural and as referring
to one out of his mind. "If any man thinks that
these matters are wholly within the grasp of the

human mind and nothing in them is beyond our
reason [daimonion]that man is irrational
[daimonan]."[87] When the orator Aeschines described a person as "like one possessed"
(daimonios), or as we would say "obsessed,"[88] he
was giving expression to the Greek characteristic of objectifying states of mind as caused
from outside. Theophrastus' "Superstitious Man,"
when he saw a madman or an epileptic, would
shudder and spit in his bosom, a magical action
to protect himself from being similarly afflicted.[89] I refer to the statement here because of
its combination of insanity with epilepsy. Some
similarities in outward behavior led the ancients
to associate the two, a mistake which modern
medicine has corrected. The ancient Greeks
spoke of a "sacred disease," apparently referring
to epilepsy, but some doctors disputed the
popular opinion that these seizures were due to
possession by a god. A group of medical writings
ascribed to Hippocrates, the "father of medicine," attributes seizures to a natural cause;
the author complains that healers "deceive men
by prescribing for them purifications and
cleansings, most of their talk turning on the
intervention of gods and demons."[90]

There were similarities in the way madness
and demon possession affected a person. "To be
demonized" meant to be mad. Plutarch provides a
description of the actions of a man feigning to
be mad (daimononti) and to be out of his mind:

> Just as they were ready to arrest him,
> an assembly of the citizens was held, and
> here Nicias, right in the midst of some
> advice that he was giving to the people,
> suddenly threw himself upon the ground, and
> after a little while, amid the silence and
> consternation which naturally prevailed,
> lifted his head, turned it about, and
> spoke in a low and trembling voice, little
> by little raising and sharpening its tones.
> And when he saw the whole audience struck
> dumb with horror, he tore off his mantle,
> rent his tunic, and leaping up half naked,
> ran towards the exit from the theatre,
> crying out that he was pursued by the
> Mothers. No man venturing to lay hands
> upon him or even to come in his way, out of
> superstitious fear, but all avoiding him,
> he ran out of the gate of the city, freely
> using all the cries and gestures that would
> become a man possessed by demons and out of
> his mind. [Thus he escaped.][91]

Our modern secular age may not be sympathetic
with the idea of assigning insanity to demon
possession but may be more sympathetic to the
practice of ascribing religious frenzy to demonic influence. "You must be possessed [demonized],
by Pan made frantic or by Hecate, or by the
Corybantes dread, and Cybele the mountain
mother."[92]

Young people of every era may be able to
identify with the mistake which forms part of
the plot of an early Greek romance. What was
really a case of lovesickness by two young
lovers was treated as a visitation of the gods
of the underworld. Soothsayers and holy men
"offered various sacrifices, poured libations,
pronounced certain unintelligible syllables in

order to appease, as they said, certain demonic powers."[93] On the ancient Greek view Eros would have been a demon, so perhaps seeing lovesickness as demonic was not so great a mistake at that!

The belief in possession led to efforts to expel demons. Similar to the ceremonies described in this romance is the cure mentioned by Plutarch: "The Magi advise those possessed by demons to recite and name over to themselves the Ephesian letters."[94] The "Ephesian letters" refers to the unintelligible formulae used in the practice of magic. Demon-possession and the practice of magic went hand-in-hand.

An example of the magical formulae used in expelling demons is provided by the Paris Magical Papyrus from about A. D. 300 but incorporating earlier material:

> For those possessed by demons, an approved charm by Pibechis. Take oil made from unripe olives, together with the plant mastagia and lotus pith, and boil it with marjoram (very colorless), saying: "Joel, Ossarthiomi, Emori, Theochipsoith, Sithemeoch, Sothe, Joe, Mimipsothiooph, Phersothi, Aeeioyo, Joe, Eochariphth: come out of such an one (and the other usual formulae)."

> But write this phylactery upon a little sheet of tin: "Jaeo, Abraothioch, Phtah, Mesentiniae, Pheoch, Jaeo, Charsoc," and hang it round the sufferer: it is of every demon a thing to be trembled at, which he fears. Standing opposite, adjure him. The adjuration is this: "I adjure thee by the god of the Hebrews Jesu, Jaba, Jae, Abraoth,

> Aia, Thoth, Ele, Elo, Aeo, Eu, Jiibaech,
> Abarmas, . . . let thy angel descend, the
> implacable one, and let him draw into cap-
> tivity the demon as he flieth around this
> creature which God formed in his holy
> paradise.

There follows a series of adjurations of the
demon by the deity. (Remember in chapter I the
mention of adjuration in exorcism.) Then the
final instructions are given:

> But I adjure thee, thou that usest this
> adjuration: the flesh of swine eat not,
> and there shall be subject unto thee every
> spirit and demon, whatsoever he be. But
> when thou adjurest, blow, sending the
> breath from above [to the feet] and from
> the feet to the face, and the demon will
> be drawn into captivity.[95]

Jewish elements, such as are found in this passage, are not unusual in the magical papyri, for
the Jews had a considerable reputation as
magicians and exorcists,[96] and magicians freely
borrowed from their competition.

The exorcist claiming to drive out demons
who is best-known to us from ancient times is
Apollonius of Tyana, who lived at the close of
the first century A. D., and not surprisingly
he was charged with magic. One notable incident
in his life occurred when a licentious youth
broke out in coarse laughter during a discourse
by Apollonius.

> Then Apollonius looked up at him and
> said: "It is not yourself that perpetrates
> this insult, but the demon, who drives you
> on without your knowing it." And in fact
> the youth was, without knowing it,

possessed by demons; for he would laugh at
things that no one else laughed at, and
then he would fall to weeping for no reason
at all, and he would talk and sing to himself. Now most people thought that it was
the boisterous humor of youth which led him
into such excesses; but he was really the
mouthpiece of a demon, though it only
seemed a drunken frolic in which on that
occasion he was indulging. Now when
Apollonius gazed on him, the ghost in him
began to utter cries of fear and rage, . .
.; and the ghost swore that he would leave
the young man alone and never take possession of any man again. But Apollonius
addressed him with anger . . . and ordered
him to quit the young man and show by a
visible sign that he had done so. "I will
throw down yonder statue," said the demon,
and pointed to one of the images . . . .
But when the statue began by moving gen-
tly, and then fell down, it would defy
anyone to describe the hubbub which arose
and the way they clapped their hands with
wonder. [The account concludes with the
young man giving up his former way of life
and taking the philosopher's cloak, model-
ling his life on that of Apollonius.][97]

Lucian of Samosata was a delightful or a

scathing satirist, depending on which side of

his satire you found yourself. The following

account takes a jab at the Platonists, who be-

lieved in an invisible supernatural realm of

forms or ideas, of which the things in this

world are imperfect copies. The main thrust of

the story, however, is to make fun of those who

readily accepted magic and superstitious stories

of the supernatural. The story gives us very

well the flavor of the first and second-century

world in Palestine and Syria where Jesus was

active. There is no reason to think that Lucian had Jesus himself in mind, for such exorcisms as he describes were common.

> "You act ridiculously," said Ion, "to doubt everything. For my part, I should like to ask you what you say to those who free possessed men from their terrors by exorcising the demons so manifestly. I need not discuss this: everyone knows about the Syrian from Palestine, the adept in it, how many he takes in hand who fall down in the light of the moon and roll their eyes and fill their mouths with foam; neverthe-less, he restores them to health and sends them away normal in mind, delivering them from their circumstances for a large fee. When he stands beside them as they lie there and asks: 'Whence came you into this body?' the patient himself is silent, but the demon answers in Greek or in the language of whatever foreign country he comes from, telling how and whence he entered into the man; whereupon, by ad-juring the demon and if he does not obey, threatening him, he drives him out. In-deed, I actually saw one coming out, black and smoky in color." "It is nothing much," I remarked, "for you, Ion, to see that kind of sight, when even the 'forms' that the father of your school, Plato, points out are plain to you, a hazy object of vision to the rest of us."98

In these accounts of Apollonius of Tyana and the Syrian from Palestine we find much that agrees with New Testament accounts of the expel-ling of demons: these parallels include the effects of demon possession on a person, in bodily actions and in voice; anger and asser-tion of authority by the healer; and the effects on the person of the departure of the demon.

Among the differences are the fee charged, the
material description of the demon, and the physical signs given of expulsion.

Our examination of Greek literature has
produced several items of information helpful in
the understanding of demonology in general and
of the New Testament references in particular.
The different ideas were fluid, and we should
not expect complete consistency. Demons were
widely recognized as intermediary beings, occu-
pying the region between earth and heaven. They
could be good or bad, and although Plato had
conceived them primarily as good, after his time
the tendency was increasingly to attribute evil
actions to them. They determined a person's
destiny and especially were responsible for ex-
ecuting punishment after death. The demons were
often identified with the souls of the deceased
who when released from the body were free to
move about and in particular to avenge wrongs
done to the deceased. The demons were also conceived as personal guardian spirits, closely
attached to a person. On the other hand, they
could be closely attached to the gods and seen
as their deputies. Much of the apparatus of
pagan religion was interpreted by philosophers
as pertaining to demons, either as inspired by
them or directed toward their appeasement. The
demons were thought to be able to take possession of human beings, causing either madness or
other irrational behavior. Magical rites and

formulae of exorcism were resorted to in order
to drive them out.

Perhaps more important than these specific
conceptions, not always fully consistent one with
another, is the impression the literature gives
of the circumstances of New Testament times.
The Greco-Roman world was very conscious of
demons. Their presence was part of the dis-
turbing world view of the time. Their presence
and activity were a challenge to Jesus and the
Christian gospel. It was a demonstration of
Jesus' divine power and victory over evil that
he could subdue the demons "with a word" and
show that they were subject to him.

This wider atmosphere was reflected in the
specific Jewish environment in which Christianity
began. To that we turn in the next chapter.

[1]Two book length studies devoted to Plutarch's demonology are Guy Soury, _La démonologie de Plutarque: Essai sur les idées religieuses et les mythes d'un Platonicien éclectique_ (Paris, 1942) and Frederick E. Brenk, _In Mist Apparelled: Religious Themes in Plutarch's Moralia and Lives_ (Leiden, 1977).

[2]Plutarch, _The Obsolescence of Oracles_ 10-15 (_Moralia_ 415A-418D). The translation is adapted from that of F. C. Babbitt, _Plutarch's Moralia_, Vol. V in Loeb Classical Library (Cambridge: Harvard University Press, 1936). Other quotations from classical authors will be taken from or based on the Loeb Classical Library.

[3]Acts 17:18 uses _daimonia_ in this sense of "divinities," with probable allusion to the charges against Socrates (Plato, _Apology_ 24B-C).

[4]_Iliad_ I.222.

[5]_Iliad_ V.438-441. Cf. III.420 where Aprodite is referred to as the _daimōn_.

[6]Isocrates I.13.

[7]Dio Cassius LIII.8.1.

[8]Aristophanes, _Wasps_ 525; Diodorus Siculus IV.3.4; Plutarch, _Table Talk_ III.7.1 (_Moralia_ 655E).

[9]_Iliad_ XVII.98f.; cf. XI.792.

[10]Herodotus V.87; cf. Homer, _Odyssey_ III. 26-28.

[11]Aeschines III.13; cf. Thucydides II.642, "hardships sent by heaven and those from the enemy"; Xenophon, _Memorabilia_ I.1.12.

[12]_Republic_ II, 382E.

[13]_Discourse_ XXXII.76.

[14]Electra 1270; cf. Xenophon, Memorabilia I.3.5.

[15]Pindar, Olympian Ode IX.110.

[16]Bacchylides, Heracles 11 (xv).35.

[17]Aeschylus, Persians 581.

[18]Aeschylus, Libation-Bearers 566.

[19]Aristophanes, Peace 585; cf. Sophocles, Antigone 376 for a "portent."

[20]Plato, Timaeus 25E.

[21]On Prophecy in Sleep II (463B).

[22]Pindar, Olympian Ode VIII.67.

[23]Herodotus I.111; Epictetus, Discourses I.xix.19.

[24]Euripides, Bacchanals 894; cf. Herodotus VII.18, "since heaven impels."

[25]Bacchylides XV.23 and XVI.117.

[26]Philemo 191.

[27]Description of Greece VIII.33.1; cf. Sophocles, Oedipus at Colonus 1443; Aristophanes, Birds 544.

[28]Works and Days 314.

[29]Homer, Iliad VIII.166; cf. Aeschylus, Seven Against Thebes 812.

[30]Odyssey XI.61.

[31]Odyssey V.396f.; cf. X.64.

[32]Laws V, 732C; for an exception in Plato, "ill fortune," cf. Greater Hippias 304B. For good fortune see Aeschylus, Persians 601f.

[33]Sophocles, Oedipus King 828.

[34]Persians 354.

[35]Works and Days 110-139. Other references to Hesiod's view are found in Plutarch, Obsolescence of Oracles 38 and Sign of Socrates 24 (Moralia 431B and 593D).

[36]Cratylus 397D-398C. Plato often employed the classification gods, demons, heroes-- Republic IV, 427B; Laws IV, 717B; VII, 801E;etc.

[37]Plutarch, Obsolescence of Oracles 10 (Moralia 415B-C); Romulus 28.8 (Lives 36).

[38]Theogony 991.

[39]Alcestis 1003; cf. Sophocles, Fragment 173.

[40]Cf. Aeschylus, Persians 620, "summon the demon [soul] of Darius."

[41]Apuleius, God of Socrates, says that the human soul is called a demon; while still in the body it is called in Latin the person's genius but after it has left the body it is called in Latin lemures. An English translation of the passage is found in The Works of Apuleius: A New Translation (London: George Bell and Sons, 1902), pp. 362ff.

[42]Passing of Peregrinus 27.

[43]Ibid. 36; cf. also Lover of Lies 29 and 31; Funerals 24.

[44]Description of Greece VI.6.8.

[45]As in the "Legend of Sleepy Hollow."

[46]Plutarch, Caesar 69.

[47]F. A. Wilford, "Daimon in Homer," Numen 12 (1965) 217-232, argues for a psychological interpretation of daimon already in Homer. If this should be accepted, then there was early precedent for the usage in Socrates and Plato.

[48]The idea of accompanying spirits itself may have been earlier, although the references cited are not unambiguous. Possibilities are Phocylides, Fragment 15, from Clement of Alexandria, Miscellanies V.14, "Now there are demons upon men . . . some to save from coming ill" followed by a line now lost which presumably mentioned some who did evil. Theognis I.161-164 may be an accompanying spirit or only "fortune." Pindar, Olympian Odes XIII.105 seems to refer to a protective spirit.

[49]Plato, Thaetetus 151A, "if my demon allow"; cf. Apology 24C; 40A; Xenophon, Memorabilia I. 1.1-4. Both Plutarch and Apuleius wrote a treatise on the demon of Socrates.

[50]Apuleius, God of Socrates, makes the identification with conscience and explains that it forbade him to do certain things but never exhorted him to the performance of anything, for Socrates did not need any one to exhort him to do good but he needed warning of danger. Plutarch makes much of Socrates' demon being a voice and not a vision--Sign of Socrates 18 (Moralia 588C).

[51]Republic X, 617C.

[52]Ibid., 620D-E.

[53]Laws X, 906A.

[54]Phaedo 107D; 108B; and 113D; the same thought is in Plutarch, Divine Vengeance 25 (Moralia 564F).

[55]Sign of Socrates 24 (Moralia 593F-594A); cf. 20 (589D).

[56]Lives of the Philosophers VII.151.

[57]Discourses I.xiv.12-14. The idea of a
personal accompanying demon was already popular
in the Hellenistic age, for the playwright
Menander (late fourth century B. C.) had said,
"Beside every man there is placed from his birth
a demon, a good guide through life's mysteries"
--Frg. 551. Plutarch, On Tranquility of Mind 15
(Moralia 474B) quotes Menander and rejects his
view in favor of Empedocles' two fates or demons
accompanying each person.

[58]Meditations V.27.

[59]Discourses III.xxii.53.

[60]Diogenes Laertius, Lives of the Philosophers VIII.32.

[61]Apology 15 (27B-E).

[62]Timaeus 40D-41D.

[63]Epinomis 984D-985B. Eusebius later sum-
marized the Greek view of the heavenly topography
this way: "They say that the heaven, and the
ether as far down as the moon, are assigned to
gods; and the parts about the moon and the
atmosphere to demons; and the region of the
earth and parts beneath the earth to souls. And
having made such a distribution they say that we
ought to worship first of all the gods of heaven
and of the ether, secondly the good demons,
thirdly the souls of the heroes, and fourthly to
propitiate the bad and wicked demons."
(Preparation for the Gospel IV.5,141c-d).

[64]Summary of Plato's view in Plutarch, Isis
and Osiris 26 (Moralia 361C). Cf. Apuleius,
God of Socrates for a similar summary about the
intermediary place of demons, with reference to
the Symposium passage quoted above; Apuleius
then develops their intermediary nature (as
well as location), "having immortality in common with the Gods of heaven and passions

in common with subordinate beings," after the fashion of Xenocrates, discussed below.

[65]See the particular development of this thought in the Christian apologists discussed in Chapter IV.

[66]Cf. Obsolescence of Oracles 38 (Moralia 431B); 48 (463E-F); 51 (438D). One member of the dialogue granted that demons were in charge of oracles but questioned that they die and that sins are theirs--16 (418E).

[67]Laws VIII, 848D; cf. Pausanias, Description of Greece I.2.5 for "a demon attendant upon Dionysus."

[68]Obsolescence of Oracles 21 (Moralia 421E).

[69]Laws IV, 713D.

[70]Statesman 271D.

[71]Plutarch includes Plato along with Empedocles, Xenocrates, Chrysippus, and Democritus (implicitly) as having bequeathed to us bad demons--Obsolescence of Oracles 17 (Moralia 419A).

[72]Plutarch, Isis and Osiris 25 (Moralia 360E).

[73]For the divine hierarchy in which demons may move up or down see the Hermetic tractate Asclepius 5.

[74]Isis and Osiris 30 (Moralia 362E and 363A); cf. 25 (360E).

[75]Isis and Osiris 26 (Moralia 361B).

[76]Apology 43.

[77]Dion II.1-3 (Lives 958).

[78]Dinner of Seven Wise Men 8 (Moralia 153A).

[79]Plutarch, Stoic Contradictions 37 (Moralia 1051C).

[80]Plutarch, Roman Questions 51 (Moralia 277A).

[81]Plutarch, On the Control of Anger 9 (Moralia 458C).

[82]Corpus Hermeticum XVI.10f.

[83]Ibid. IX.3.

[84]Asclepius 33; 5.2f.

[85]Corpus Hermeticum IV.8.

[86]Ibid. I.23.

[87]Xenophon, Memorabilia I.1.9.

[88]Aeschines I.41; cf. in a stronger sense Euripides, Phoenician Maidens 888.

[89]Characters 16.

[90]Hippocrates, The Sacred Disease 1-3.

[91]Marcellus 20.5f. (Lives 309).

[92]Euripides, Hippolytus 141ff.

[93]Xenophon of Ephesus, An Ephesian Tale I.5.

[94]Table Talk V (Moralia 706E).

[95]Paris Magical Papyrus lines 3,007-3,085; trans. from C. K. Barrett, The New Testament Background (New York: Macmillan, 1957), pp. 31-33. The whole passage is studied by W. L. Knox as an example of "Jewish Liturgical Exorcism," in Harvard Theological Review 31(1938)191-203. Magic was used to protect from demons (Paris Magical Papyrus 2700 ff.); a list of the different kinds of things used to ward off demons is found in Eusebius, Preparation for the Gospel IV.1,131b-132b.

[96]Acts 13:6-11; 19:13;16.

[97]Philostratus, Life of Apollonius IV.20; cf. another case in III.38 and its description of the effects of possession so that the possessed spoke with another voice; other stories in II.4; IV.10 (a similar story in the Christian apocryphal Acts of Peter 11); IV.25; IV.44.

[98]Lucian, Lover of Lies 16; cf. 17 and 31.

CHAPTER III

JEWISH VIEWS ON DEMONOLOGY

The book of 1 Enoch, in a passage coming
from perhaps the early second century B. C.,
contains an account of the origin of demons.[1]
This pseudepigraphal book gave an interpretation of Genesis 6:1-4, which reads in the
Authorized Version as follows:

> . . . . The sons of God saw the
> daughters of men that they were fair; and
> they took them wives of all which they
> chose. . . . There were giants in the
> earth in those days; and also after that,
> when the sons of God came in unto the
> daughters of men, and they bare children
> to them, the same became mighty men which
> were of old, men of renown.

The author of 1 Enoch understood the "sons of
God," as the Hebrew may be understood, as angels
and offered the following reinterpretation of
Genesis:

> And it came to pass when the children of
> men had multiplied that in those days were
> born unto them beautiful and comely daugh-
> ters. And the angels, the children of
> heaven, saw and lusted after them, and said
> to one another: "Come, let us choose us
> wives from among the children of men and
> beget us children.[2]

The angels were rebuked by God for what they had
done. It was explained that human beings, who
are mortal and die, reproduce themselves sex-
ually so as to maintain their numbers on the
earth, but the angels (called "Watchers of
heaven") are spiritual and immortal and have no
need of engaging in human conduct.

69

> Therefore I [God] have not appointed
> wives for you; for as for the spiritual
> ones of the heaven, in heaven is their
> dwelling. And now, the giants, who are
> produced from the spirits and flesh, shall
> be called evil spirits upon the earth, and
> on the earth shall be their dwelling. Evil
> spirits have proceeded from their bodies;
> because they are born from men and from the
> holy Watchers is their beginning and primal
> origin; they shall be evil spirits on
> earth, and evil spirits shall they be
> called. . . . And the spirits of the
> giants afflict, oppress, destroy, attack,
> do battle, and work destruction on the
> earth, and cause trouble: they take no
> food, but nevertheless hunger and thirst,
> and cause offences. And these spirits shall
> rise up against the children of men and
> against the women, because they proceeded
> from them. From the days of the slaughter
> and destruction and death of the giants,
> from the souls of whose flesh the spirits,
> having gone forth, shall destroy without
> incurring judgment--thus shall they destroy
> until the day of consummation, the great
> judgment.[3]

Thus the author of 1 Enoch saw evil spirits (or
demons) as being the spirits of the giants which
resulted from the intercourse of angels with
women. These evil spirits tempt men to evil,[4]
accuse the fallen,[5] and punish the condemned.[6]
The author of 1 Enoch, however, also insists
that man is himself the source of moral evil.[7]

Old Testament

The Greek translation of the Old Testament,
the Septuagint, had already understood the "sons
of God" of Genesis 6 as angels. The translators
rendered Genesis 6:2, "the angels of God saw the

daughters of men," although they kept the literal "sons of God" in verse 4.

Not a great deal is said about demonic
beings in the Old Testament. "Satan," the
"Adversary," is mentioned in only three passages. In Job 1-2 he is a member of the divine
court, an accuser of men. Similarly in
Zechariah 3:1f. Satan accuses the high priest
Joshua, but is rebuked by the Lord. In both
passages Satan has limited powers under the Lord
and functions to test the righteousness of one
favored by the Lord, and in both cases the Lord
justifies the person accused. According to
1 Chronicles 21:1 Satan incited David to trans-
gress by numbering the people of Israel.[8]

Isaiah 14 and Ezekiel 28 are often taken as
referring, either ultimately or by analogy, to
Satan. The passages, however, are clearly referring in their context to the king of Babylon and
the king of Tyre, respectively, and are not
talking about the origin of the devil. These
two chapters are part of the biblical basis for
John Milton's description of Satan in his great
epic, Paradise Lost.

> The infernal Serpent; he it was, whose
>   guile,
> Stirred up with envy and revenge, deceived
> The mother of mankind; what time his pride
> Had cast him out from heaven, with all his
>   host
> Of rebel angels; by whose aid, aspiring
> To set himself in glory above his peers,
> He trusted to have equaled the Most High,

If he opposed; and, with ambitious aim
Against the throne and monarchy of God,
Raised impious war in heaven, and battle
        proud,
With vain attempt. Him the Almighty Power
Hurled headlong flaming from the ethereal
        sky,
With hideous ruin and combustion, down
To bottomless perdition; there to dwell
In adamantine chains and penal fire,
Who durst defy the Omnipotent to arms.

Milton has the proud Satan defiantly declare to
Beelzebul:

"Fallen cherub, to be weak is miserable,
Doing or suffering; but of this be sure,
To do aught good never will be our task,
But ever to do ill our sole delight,
As being the contrary to his high will
Whom we resist. If then his providence
Out of our evil seek to bring forth good,
Our labor must be to pervert that end,
And out of good still to find means of evil,
Which ofttimes may succeed, so as perhaps
Shall grieve him, if I fail not, and disturb
His inmost counsels from their destined aim.
. . . .

. . . . Farewell, happy fields,
Where joy for ever dwells! Hail, horrors!
        hail
Infernal world! and thou profoundest hell,
Receive thy new possessor--one who brings
A mind not to be changed by place or time:
The mind is its own place, and in itself
Can make a heaven of hell, a hell of heaven.
What matter where, if I be still the same,
And what I should be; all but less than he
Whom thunder hath made greater? Here at
        least
We shall be free: the Almighty hath not
        built
Here for his envy, will not drive us hence:
Here we may reign secure, and, in my choice,
To reign is worth ambition, though in hell;
Better to reign in hell, than serve in
        heaven."9

Milton created the powerful poetry, but he did
not invent the interpretation. It was well
established in the Christian tradition. But we
should recognize that it is an interpretation of
the biblical materials and not anything stated
in the Bible. Our theological constructions and
interpretations of the Scriptures should not be
confused with the biblical data itself.

As for other evil spirits, the Old
Testament also refers to an "evil spirit from
the Lord" which tormented Saul with mental illness.[10] The Old Testament further has occasional
references to hairy or goat-like creatures (cf.
the Greek satyrs) inhabiting deserted places;
the Greek translators designated them <u>daimonia</u>.[11]
It was anciently believed that he-goats were
possessed with demons, and this seems to account
for the identification of demons with goat-like
creatures. The Greek Old Testament, in addition,
refers to demons which cause terror at night or
in the blazing noonday sun.[12] More significant
for later Jewish and Christian usage was the
declaration that "all the gods of the Gentiles
are demons."[13] Thus when Israel turned to pagan
gods, it was said that the people had "sacri-
ficed to demons."[14] The statement of Isaiah
65:11, "They set a table for the demon and fill
cups of mixed wine for Tyche" provided the background for Paul's sharply formulated contrast in
1 Corinthians 10:21, "You cannot drink the cup
of the Lord and the cup of demons. You cannot

partake of the table of the Lord and the table
of demons." In the preceding verse Paul had
repeated the declaration of Deuteronomy 32:17 in
saying that pagans sacrifice to demons and not
to God.

From these beginnings developed an elab-
orate speculation about demons in intertestamental or post-biblical Jewish writings.

Intertestamental Literature

The book of Jubilees, a rewriting of
Genesis, alluded to the 1 Enoch story of the sin
of the divine beings with women.[15] Jubilees
also refers to sacrifice offered to demons, the
standard interpretation of pagan religion,
especially in contexts dealing with Jewish
apostasy.[16] The most distinctive feature of the
demonology of Jubilees is found in chapter 10.
In response to the prayer of Noah, God ordered
all the evil spirits to be bound. Mastema, the
chief of the spirits, however, pled that "if
some of them are not left to me, I shall not be
able to execute the power of my will on the sons
of men; for these are for corruption and leading
astray before my judgment, for great is the
wickedness of the sons of men." Consequently,
one-tenth of the evil spirits were left subject
to Satan on earth, and the remainder were bound
in the place of condemnation.[17] The good angels
taught Noah about the seductions of evil spirits
and medicines to cure the illnesses caused by
them. The book of Jubilees is full of references

to the evil which these spirits seduced men to
do in the Old Testament.

> And the prince Mastema exerted himself
> to do all this [transgression and unclean-
> ness], and he sent forth other spirits,
> those which were under his hand, to do all
> manner of wrong and sin, and all manner of
> transgression, to corrupt and destroy, and
> to shed blood upon the earth.[18]

God "placed spirits in authority [over the
nations] to lead them astray from him. But over
Israel he did not appoint any angel or spirit,
for he alone is their ruler."[19] The author,
however, looked forward to an age when "there
shall be no Satan nor any evil destroyer."[20]

Several of these ideas find further elaboration in other intertestamental literature,
and new ideas were introduced. For instance,
other explanations of the origin of the demonic
powers are to be found in the pseudepigraphal
literature. The book of 2 Enoch refers to a
rebellion of the angels, without any reference
to Genesis 6:

> One from out of the order of angels,
> having turned away with the order that was
> under him, conceived an impossible thought,
> to place his throne higher than the clouds
> above the earth, that he might become equal
> in rank to my [God's] power. And I threw
> him out from the height with his angels,
> and he was flying in the air continuously
> above the bottomless.[21]

This already sounds very much like Milton. Some
such beliefs as those in Jubilees and 2 Enoch
about a rebellion by angels and their expulsion

from the presence of God into a place of punishment appears to be behind 2 Peter 2:4 and Jude 6.
The latter's statement about "did not keep their
own position but left their proper dwelling" has
often been referred to the account of Genesis 6,
but might as easily, or even more credibly be
referred to such a rebellion as 2 Enoch recounts.
Jubilees would further explain how some evil
spirits are already bound over for punishment
but some are still active.

The Life of Adam associated the fall of
angels with jealousy of man's position in
creation:

> The devil replied, "Adam, ... It is
> for thy sake that I have been hurled from
> that place. . . . When God blew into thee
> the breath of life and thy face and like-
> ness was made in the image of God, Michael
> also brought thee and made us worship thee
> in the sight of God. . . . And I said to
> him, 'Why dost thou urge me? I will not
> worship an inferior and younger being than
> I. I am his senior in the creation, before
> he was made was I already made. It is his
> duty to worship me.' When the angels who
> were under me heard this, they refused to
> worship him. . . . And God the Lord was
> wroth with me and banished me and my angels
> from our glory; and on thy account were we
> expelled from our abode into this world and
> hurled on the earth. And straightway we
> were overcome with grief, since we had been
> spoiled of so great glory. And we were
> grieved when we saw thee in such joy and
> luxury. And with guile I cheated thy wife
> and caused thee to be expelled through her
> doing from thy joy and luxury, as I have
> been driven out of my glory.[22]

The intertestamental literature provides a

rich vocabulary for the prince of the evil demons. Mastema was the favorite name in Jubilees. He is, of course, the devil: "The Devil is the evil spirit of lower places [earthly order]."[23] The plural Satans is used in 1 Enoch 40:7 for those who "accuse them who dwell on the earth." Another name frequently encountered is that of "Beliar, the great prince, the king of this world who has ruled it since it came into being."[24] Beliar and the wicked angels are often met in the Testaments of the Twelve Patriarchs. The variant Belial is found in the Qumran literature and Damascus Document.[25]

The name Asmodeus belongs to the evil demon in the book of Tobit, the most striking story in the Old Testament Apocrypha. Tobias, the son of the righteous Tobit, was sent on a journey to collect some money which his father had left in trust with a friend. Tobias was accompanied on the trip by a man who was actually the angel Raphael in human disguise. On their way they stopped at Ecbatana, where lived Raguel, a kinsman of Tobit. Raguel had a beautiful daughter named Sarah, who had had a series of unfortunate experiences. Sarah had been engaged seven times, but each man had died in the bridal chamber before the marriage was consummated, killed by the demon Asmodeus, who loved Sarah and would not let anyone approach her.[26] Before Tobias and Raphael arrived in Ecbatana, they had stopped at the Tigris river and caught a fish.

The angel instructed Tobias to cut open the fish and take the heart, liver, and gall out and save them, with the promise "if a demon or evil spirit gives trouble to any one, you make a smoke from these before the man or woman and that person will never be troubled again."[27] Tobias found Sarah very attractive and desired to marry her, but was fearful, because seven others had died attempting to marry her, but the angel Raphael reassured him that if he took live ashes of incense and burned some of the heart and liver of the fish, the smoke would drive away the demon.[28] I do not know about demons, but I would think the odor of the insides of a fish dead for several days would drive most nearly anything away. Well, it surely worked on Asmodeus. "When the demon smelled the odor he fled to the remotest parts of Egypt and the angel bound him."[29] Many motifs of folklore about demons are combined in this tale: a demon's love for a beautiful woman, the mysterious and dangerous qualities of a new bride, the use of magic as a protection against demons, and the terminology of "binding" a demon.

The Testaments of the Twelve Patriarchs uses the word "spirit" in the sense of "evil spirit" in reference to various sinful impulses, e.g. "spirit of fornication," "spirit of envy," etc. There are "seven spirits of deceit" appointed against man.[30] With this moralizing and internalizing of the idea of the demonic went a corresponding emphasis on the attitudes and conduct which would defeat evil.

> Fear ye the Lord, and love your neighbor; and even though the spirits of Beliar claim you to afflict you with every evil, yet shall they not have dominion over you . . . . For he that feareth God and loveth his neighbor cannot be smitten by the spirit of Beliar, being shielded by the fear of God.[31]

"For if a man flee to the Lord, the evil spirit runneth away from him."[32] On the other hand, those who have served evil desires, will continue to be punished by them after this life: "For when the soul departs troubled, it is tormented by the evil spirit which also it served in lusts and evil works."[33] In a similar vein, a principal function of the demons in 1 Enoch is indicated by their designation as "angels of punishment."[34]

Quite similar to the perspective of the Testaments is the teaching of the Qumran documents (popularly known as the Dead Sea Scrolls) about the two spirits given to each person. The Rule of the Community (or Manual of Discipline) says the following:

> From the God of Knowledge comes all that is and shall be . . . . And he allotted unto man two spirits that he should walk in them until the time of his visitation; they are the spirits of truth and perversity. . . . Dominion over all the sons of righteousness is in the hand of the Prince of light. All dominion over the sons of perversity is in the hand of the Angel of darkness. . . . And these are the ways of

> these spirits in the world. It is of the
> spirit of truth to enlighten the heart of
> man. . . . And to it belong the spirit of
> humility and forbearance, of abundant mercy
> and eternal goodness, of understanding and
> intelligence, and almighty wisdom with
> faith in all the words of God and trust in
> his abundant grace. . . . But to the spirit
> of perversity belong cupidity, and slack-
> ness in the service of righteousness,
> impiety and falsehood, pride and haughti-
> ness, falsity and deceit, cruelty and
> abundant wickedness . . . . But in his
> mysteries of understanding and in his glo-
> rious wisdom God has set an end for the
> existence of perversity; and at the time of
> the visitation he will destroy it for ever
> . . . . Till now the spirits of truth and
> perversity battle in the hearts of every
> man; they walk in wisdom or folly.[35]

The closely related Damascus Document gives the
following protection against demons: "On the
day on which a man undertakes to be converted to
the Law of Moses, the angel of hostility will
depart from him if he fulfills his promises."[36]
That demons incite men to sin is an important
difference between later Jewish demonology and
primitive religion and Greek views.[37]

Demonic activity was expected to continue
until God overthrows evil. It was a common
feature of the expectation concerning the messianic age that the power of demons would be
broken at that time. God's Elect One will sit
on his throne of glory and judge "Azazel, all
his associates, and all his hosts in the name of
the Lord of Spirits."[38] The Testaments of the
Twelve Patriarchs contain several statements

about the Lord binding Beliar and overcoming the
evil spirits. "And after these things there
shall arise unto you the Lord himself, the light
of righteousness . . . . He shall redeem all
the captivity of the sons of men from Beliar;
and every spirit of deceit shall be trodden
down."[39] At the end time "all the spirits of
deceit shall be given to be trodden under foot,
and men shall rule over wicked spirits."[40]

> And he shall open the gates of paradise,
> and shall remove the threatening sword
> against Adam. And he shall give to the
> saints to eat from the tree of life, and
> the spirit of holiness shall be on them.
> And Beliar shall be bound by him, and he
> shall give power to his children to tread
> upon the evil spirits.[41]

Another document, usually dated to the beginning
of the first century, expects God's kingdom to
"appear throughout all his creation, and then
Satan shall be no more, and sorrow shall depart
with him."[42]

Philo and Josephus

Hellenistic Jewish authors of the first
century who wrote in Greek show an awareness of
the Jewish ideas on demons, but their terminology reflects Greek word usage. Hence, our
consideration of the writings of Philo and
Josephus will serve as a review of the material
on the meanings of the words for demons in Greek
as well as providing a more immediate context
for New Testament teaching.

Philo, the Jewish philosopher from

Alexandria, used "demon," as did pagan authors,
in reference to deities. Whether there was the
pejorative Jewish meaning present or only the
ordinary pagan reference to a supernatural power
cannot always be determined. Certainly there
was nothing negative when Philo was quoting a
Greek author's reference to "a certain demon or
a god."[43] The same would seem true when Philo
referred to the name of the Agathos Daimōn.[44]
There is the possibility of Jewish undertones
when Philo spoke of a pillar in honor of "some
daimonion" (deity) which the natives worshipped,[45] referred to the god Ares as a demon, and
spoke of those who "invent marine deities";[46]
but since Philo had a Greek education and wrote
for Greeks, even these passages may simply reflect ordinary Greek usage.

Such ordinary Greek usage would be favored
by the way Philo reproduced the usage of demon
for anything superhuman or marvellous: "superhuman skill"[47] and "truth is marvellously
beautiful."[48] Similarly he could use the word
for demon in reference to fate (or misfortune)[49]
or destiny.[50] Furthermore, Philo could speak of
the stars as "divine or demonic natures"[51]
according to the common Hellenistic conception of
the stars as gods.

Another ordinary Greek usage of demon reflected in Philo is that of souls of the deceased
who avenged the deceased. Philo in one passage
refers to "demons [in this case, ghostly avengers]

of [a person's] dead wife."[52]

The most distinctive use of demons in Philo, however, and the meaning which apparently was most significant to him, was as equivalent to the biblical word "angels," further equated by him also (in good Greek fashion) with souls. Thus he speaks of two kinds of bodiless souls: some enter into bodies, but others exist on high. The latter, he explains, were called by the Greeks heroes, and Moses called them angels.[53] Philo's treatise On the Giants gave him the fullest opportunity to correlate the Jewish and Greek ideas of demons. He does so in commenting on Genesis 6:2: "It is Moses' custom to give the name of angels to those whom other philosophers call daimonas, souls that is which fly and hover in the air."[54] He avoided taking the "sons of God" in Genesis 6, however, as angels who had intercourse with women.[55] The implications of his synthesis of Greek and Jewish ideas come out in the following statement:

> If you realize that souls, demons, and angels are but different names for the same one underlying object, you will cast from you that most grievous burden, the fear of demons [or superstition]. The common usage of men is to give the name of demon to good and bad demons alike, and the name of soul to good and bad souls.[56]

So also there are good and bad angels.[57] Therefore, Philo accepted an intermediate class of spiritual beings which might be good and serve God, or be bad and oppose him. He testified to the ordinary Greek usage at the beginning of the first century by which demons might refer to either or both kinds. Philo's synthesis did not prevail, however, because Christian usage came to apply angels to the good beings in God's service and demons to the evil rebels. Occasionally Christians made reference to bad angels, as when the New Testament speaks of "the Devil and his angels,"[58] but the New Testament never speaks of demons in a good sense.[59]

Josephus, the Jewish historian, has if anything an even more varied usage of the "demon" family of words but lacks a distinctive explanation comparable to Philo's. He can use daimonion to mean "the Deity," or "the divine."[60] This divine power is particularly the dispenser of fate. "In truth the divine power [daimonion] had given [Herod] a great many instances of good fortune, even more than he had hoped for, in external affairs, but in his own home it was his fate to meet with the greatest misfortune."[61] Or the word may mean the destiny, fate, or misfortune itself.[62] Often it is difficult to decide whether one should translate in the personal sense, "the Deity," or impersonally, "Fortune."[63] My victory, Josephus says, "that day would have been complete, had I not been thwarted by some demon," or should we say "misfortune"?[64] Other places where there is ambiguity between a personal demon or impersonal fate[65] have in common that the occurrence is a misfortune. Thus it is not surprising that the word was also used for a demonic, evil spirit without any qualification[66] or for what opposed one's plans.[67]

Josephus could use demon for personal good spirits, but perhaps it is significant that when he does he qualifies them as "good demons."[68] He makes reference in a neutral way to the daimonion which gave communications to Socrates.[69] His most frequent usage of demons is in reference to the souls of the departed,[70] and popular belief is shown in that the reference is usually to avenging spirits.

Evil spirits could enter a person and take possession of him, but they could also be driven out. Thus Josephus uses daimonia to interpret the biblical "evil spirit" that tormented Saul and that was driven away by David's music.[71] Josephus knew of "the so-called daimonia--in other words, the spirits of wicked men which enter the living and kill them unless aid is forthcoming" and also of the root of a plant which possessed the power of expelling such demons "if merely applied to the patients."[72] Josephus, furthermore, repeated the common Jewish view that "God granted Solomon knowledge of the art used against demons for the benefit and healing of men."[73] He proceeded to recount an instance of exorcism which has features comparable to those found in the pagan environment.

>And this kind of cure is of very great power among us to this day, for I have seen a certain Eleazar, a countryman of mine, in the presence of Vespasian, his sons, tribunes and a number of other soldiers, free men possessed by demons, and this was the manner of the cure: he put in the nose of the possessed man a ring which had under its seal one of the roots prescribed by Solomon, and then, as the man smelled it, drew out the demon through his nostrils, and, when the man at once fell down, adjured the demon never to come back into him, speaking Solomon's name and reciting the incantations which he had composed. Then, wishing to convince the bystanders and prove to them that he had this power, Eleazar placed a cup or foot-basin full of water a little way off and commended the demon, as it went out of the man, to over-turn it and make known to the spectators that he had left the man. And when this was done, the understanding and wisdom of Solomon were clearly revealed.[74]

The difference in procedure between this exorcism and Jesus' methods of driving out evil spirits should be obvious.

Rabbinic Literature

Rabbinic literature was all written later than the New Testament, but it often preserves teachings and traditions earlier than the time of writing. Thus rabbinic literature deserves consideration here, both as part of the possible background of New Testament times and as a completion of the picture of early Jewish thought on the subject of demons.

That "demons are the descendants of the fallen angels from their union with the daughters

of man, nothing but a slight trace thereof re-
mains in rabbinic literature"; that they are
"seducers to idolatry and other transgressions
does not occur at all."[75] A commonly repeated
view was that demons were a special creation of
God on the sixth day. Already in the Mishnah,
codified in the late second century of our era,
the destroying angels are listed among the
creations of the sixth day.[76] A later explanation was that "after the souls were created, the
Sabbath" came and prevented the completion of
the work of creation, "and so they remained
without bodies."[77] Yet another explanation, of
a more mythological kind, attributed the demons
to the union of Adam with female spirits and Eve
with male spirits.[78] The theme of rebellion,
but with another locus, recurs in the explanation
that some involved in the building of the tower
of Babel (Genesis 11:1-9) were turned into demons
as a punishment for their pride.[79]

The nature of the demons was the subject of
considerable speculation among the rabbis. The
principal passage on their nature repeats a
fairly early tradition:

> Our rabbis taught: Six things are said
> concerning demons: in regard to three,
> they are like the ministering angels; in re-
> gard to three, like human beings. "In
> regard to three they are like the ministering
> angels": they have wings like the minister-
> ing angels; and they fly from one end of
> the world to the other like the ministering
> angels; and they know what will happen like
> the ministering angels. . . . And in

regard to three, they are like human beings": they eat and drink like human beings; they propagate like human beings; and they die like human beings.[80]

Thus the demons were viewed as spiritual beings but with certain human-like characteristics. They are intermediary beings, inferior in some respects to angels, but in other respects superior to human beings. Another passage speaks of three classes of demons: those angel-like, those human-like, and those animal-like.[81] That would correspond to the different forms in which they manifested themselves and systematize some of the diverse reports about them. As spirits, they are ordinarily invisible. "They change their appearance to any likeness they please; and they see, but themselves are not seen."[82] They are able to appear particularly in human form and to cast a shadow.[83] They can indeed appear in many forms and change into many colors.[84] Magical practices can make them appear, as well as make them disappear.

> If one wants to discover them [demons], let him take sifted ashes and sprinkle around his bed, and in the morning he will see something like the footprints of a cock. If one wishes to see them, let him take the afterbirth of a black she-cat, the offspring of a black she-cat, the firstborn of a firstborn, let him roast it in fire and grind it to powder, and then let him put some into his eyes, and he will see them.

Someone who would do that deserves to see a demon!

> R. Bibi b. Abaye did so, saw them, and
> came to harm. [The story has a good ending,
> for] The scholars, however, prayed for him
> and he recovered.[85]

The same passage speaks about the demons as being
present at the debates of scholars in the rabbinic academies. I have heard some debates
among scholars and professors where I would not
doubt that demons were present, if not indeed
taking an active part!

The number of the demons was considered to
be exceedingly large, so much so that they fill
the whole world. The same passage from the
Babylonian Talmud from which I have been quoting
above (bBerakoth 6a) also speaks about their
number and some of their activities.

> If the eye had power to see them, no
> creature could endure the demons. Abaye
> says: They are more numerous than we are
> and they surround us like the ridge round
> a field. R. Huna says: Every one among us
> has 1,000 on his left hand and 10,000 on
> his right hand. . . . Fatigue in the knees
> comes from them. The wearing out of the
> clothes of the scholars is due to their
> rubbing against them. The bruising of the
> feet comes from them.[86]

Now you know why your clothes wear out! And you
thought your sore feet came from jogging!

Passages cited earlier from the pseudepigraphical literature indicated that the demons
were active in the air and on the earth.
Rabbinic literature specifies places and times
where they are particularly active. For instance, they especially frequented isolated

wilderness areas and ruins.[87] Places of cere-
monial or other impurity were frequented by
demons, particularly cited a number of times are
toilets.[88] Unlike some other views we have encountered, water was also a place where the
demons were thought to dwell; and that meant
that the top portion of water drawn from a well
should be poured off before it was drunk.[89]

The demons were especially active in dark
places, so even familiar houses and fields could
be dangerous at night time. If one slept alone
in a house, he might be seized by Lilith, the
most frequently named female demon.[90] It was
even forbidden to greet another at night, for
fear he might be a demon.[91] The demons would
try to attack scholars at night.[92] There seems
to be the ordinary human fear of the dark and
the unknown operative here. An evil spirit is
said to show himself and do harm to a person
alone; to two persons he may show himself; to
three persons he will not even show himself. And
it is stated that a torch is the equivalent of
two persons, and a moonlight is equal to three
persons.[93] The crowing of the cock in early
morning would drive a demon away.[94] The evening
of Wednesday and the Sabbath were times of
special demon activity.[95] Actually any time of
day could be an awesome time, such as morning
and midday.[96]

The demons, although belonging to the kingdom of Satan, are part of God's creation

and stand ultimately in the service of God who
gives them their power.[97] The emphasis, as
might be expected, is on their negative activities. The intertestamental literature furnished
statements about the demons bringing troubles
and misfortunes into the world; that blame is
assigned to them also in rabbinic literature.[98]
These include seduction to sin,[99] causing illness[100] and madness,[101] impoverishing men,[102]
and even killing.[103] They often imitate divine
activity. For instance, God speaks through
dreams, and so do the demons, but they do so
falsely.[104] As ministers of God they carry out
punishment due to men for their sins.[105]

      There is, on the other hand, another side
to the activity of demons. They could be sum-
moned to the aid of men. Solomon is quite
prominent in rabbinic literature as one who knew
the secrets by which to obtain mastery over
demons. Solomon ruled over the denizens of the
upper world [demons] as well as the lower.[106]
Another view was that "Before Solomon sinned he
ruled over the demons. After he sinned, he
brought sixty warriors to protect his couch from
the terror by night."[107] Solomon's servant
Benaiahu captured Ashmedai [Asmodeus], the prince
of demons, with a chain and a ring, each of which
had graven on it the Divine Name. The demon's
help was enlisted in the building of the temple.[108]
Several of the rabbis too were believed to have
authority over the demons: e.g. Johanan ben

Zakkai.[109]   Instructions were occasionally given
about how to secure the services of demons.   One
rabbi fasted and spent the night in a cemetery
so an unclean spirit might rest upon him and
enable him to foretell the future.[110]   It was
forbidden to consult demons on the Sabbath[111]--
at least one day belongs to the Lord!

Magic was often bound up with the control
of demons, and it was this which gave Solomon
his reputation as the source of Jewish magic.
One passage refers to a distinction between
magic worked through the agency of demons and a
sorcerer who worked by pure enchantment without
outside help.[112]   Generally the magic was invoked for the negative purpose of dispelling the
demon or his effects.   There is a reference to
burning incense to a demon (which was idolatry)
as a charm.[113]   Reference may be made to a passage in the Talmud which gives a list of charms
to recite for various illnesses.   One of these
reads, "Against a demon one should say thus:
'Thou wast closed up; closed up wast thou.
Cursed, broken, and destroyed be "son of clay,
son of defilement, son of filth."'"[114]   Amulets
might be worn to ward off demons.[115]   The blow-
ing of trumpets was supposed to exorcise a
demon.[116]

More often the rabbinic literature speaks
of more spiritual means of protection against
the influence of demons.   Just to be a part of
the covenant people of Israel was itself

important. According to one passage the prince
of Gehenna voraciously demanded multitudes of
victims, but God would not give him the seed of
Isaac. Rather God said, "I have whole companies
of heathens whom I will give you."[117] When the
tabernacle was built by Moses and the priestly
blessing pronounced, the spell of the evil eye
was broken.[118] God himself was seen as a shield
for his people.[119] His angels also would afford
them protection against demons.[120] The word of
God was itself a protection.[121] Particularly
the part of scripture known as the Shema, the
Jewish confession of faith,[122] was recommended,
for every Jew would know it: "If one recites
the Shema upon his bed, the demons keep away
from him."[123] The name of God was effective:
"By the power of His name I put to flight the
harmful demons and the destroying angels."[124]
Fulfilling the commandments was another sure
protection against the demons.[125] Prayer was a
powerful weapon available to the righteous man.
The story was told of a demon who was haunting a
schoolhouse. He appeared in the guise of a
seven-headed dragon. Every time the rabbi fell
on his knees in prayer one head fell off.[126]
This may remind us of Jesus' statement that "This
kind cannot be driven out by anything but prayer"
Mark 9:29). One of my teachers used to remind
his students as they were preparing for exams,
however, that the demon of ignorance was not the
kind that came out by prayer.

Summary

      Jewish literature does not present, any
more than does Greek, a complete and consistent
doctrine of demons. Various explanations were
offered about their origin: a special creation,
angels who rebelled in heaven, souls of giants
who resulted from the intercourse of angels with
women, descendants of Adam from his intercourse
with spirits, souls punished for the rebellion
at the tower of Babel. Their nature was seen as
spiritual, but yet with certain human characteristics inconsistent with a non-bodily nature.
They are numerous and specially active at certain times and places, but capable of acting at
any time and place. They were powerful, but
aided by human desires and weaknesses. A bewil-
dering variety of names was given to certain
demons and their leader, of which we have barely
given a sampling. They cause evil, yet sometimes came into existence or became evil because
of sin. There was some tendency to a psychological interpretation, a personifying of evil.
Demons are ultimately servants of God, but in
other contexts they are identified with the gods
of pagan idolatry. So, they are servants of God,
yet enemies of God. They work havoc in his
world and accuse his servants before him, yet
they punish men for sins. God's people resist
them, yet sometimes use them to do their bidding.
Magic was not approved of, but was effective, at
least in the hands of certain individuals. There

are antidotes against the demons' activity:
the word of God, keeping the commandments, and
prayer. There was a strong conviction about and
earnest expectation for an age in which Satan
would be bound and his power broken. That is
the part with the most important contact with
Christianity.

The inconsistencies are not as great as
this summary makes them appear. Nevertheless,
it was mainly in early Christian literature that
a more consistent doctrine of demons was
achieved. This was done by selection and combination of ideas to be found in the Jewish and
Greek worlds in which early Christianity began
and grew up. And of course, Christianity
offered the conviction that the messianic age
in which the power of Satan had received a
decisive setback had begun.

[1]In addition to the general bibliography
see Kaufmann Kohler, "Demonology," The Jewish
Encyclopedia, Vol. IV (New York: Funk and
Wagnalls, 1910), pp. 514-520, and Herman L.
Strack and Paul Billerbeck, Kommentar zum Neuen
Testament aus Talmud und Midrasch, Vol. IV
(Munich: C. H. Beck, 1961), pp. 501-535, for
the subject of this chapter, although both treat
primarily the rabbinic literature; other sources
briefly in John J. Gunther, St. Paul's Opponents
and Their Background (Leiden: Brill, 1973), pp.
196-198, 205-206.

[2]1 Enoch 6:1f. Quotations from the Pseudepigrapha are taken from R. H. Charles, Apocrypha
and Pseudepigrapha of the Old Testament, Vol. II
(Oxford: Clarendon Press, 1913). More recent
translations are now available in James H.
Charlesworth, The Old Testament Pseudepigrapha
(Garden City: Doubleday, 1983).

[3]1 Enoch 15:7-16:1; cf. 106:13-17.

[4]1 Enoch 69:4-6.

[5]1 Enoch 40:7.

[6]1 Enoch 53:3; 56:1.

[7]1 Enoch 98:4f.

[8]2 Samuel 24:1 has the Lord inciting David,
so apparently Satan was the instrument of the
Lord in testing David.

[9]John Milton, Paradise Lost I.34-49; 157-
168; 249-263. Lines 367-375 repeat the Jewish
view that the demons led mankind into idolatry.

[10]1 Samuel 16:14ff.; 19:9.

[11]Isaiah 13:21; 34:14; cf. Baruch 4:35. The
Hebrew is se'irim ("hairy beings"), which occurs
also in 2 Chronicles 11:15 and Leviticus 17:7;

Azazel (Leviticus 16:10f.) perhaps belongs to this class.

[12]Psalms 91:6, Greek.

[13]Psalms 96:5, Greek; the Hebrew says "idols." See W. A. L. Emslie, The Mishnah on Idolatry (Cambridge: Cambridge University Press, 1911), pp. 42f.

[14]Deuteronomy 32:17; cf. Psalms 106:37; Isaiah 65:3; Baruch 4:7. The Hebrew is shedim. For the identification by the Greeks of a demon with the God whom it served see Plutarch, Obsolescence of Oracles 21 (Moralia 421B) and our discussion in chapter II.

[15]Jubilees 4:22; 5:1. The interpretation of the "sons of God" as angels was quite common: 2 Enoch 18; Josephus, Antiquities I.73; Testament of Reuben 5:6 understands the "sons of God" as angels but has them take human form; Philo, On the Giants XIII.58 is aware of the mystical interpretation but rejects it whereas his Questions in Genesis I.92 is based on the understanding "angels and women" but indicates "sons of God" often refers to virtuous men and contrasts "paternal virtue" with "maternal depravity"; see chapter IV for Christian references. Rabbinic literature rejected the view that there was sexual intercourse between angels and women--Louis Ginzberg, The Legends of the Jews, Vol. V (Philadelphia: Jewish Publication Society, 1955), pp. 108, 153-156. The Jew Trypho in Justin, Dialogue with Trypho 79 considered it blasphemy that angels sinned and revolted from God.

[16]Jubilees 1:11; 22:17; cf. 1 Enoch 19:1; 99:7.

[17]If the reconstruction of a (presumably Jewish) papyrus prayer against evil spirits is correct, then protection was required even against spirits in the abyss: Pierre Benoit,

"Fragment d'une prière contre les esprits impurs?" Revue Biblique 58(1951), pp. 549-565.

[18]Jubilees 11:5. See also 7:27; 10:1; 11:4; 12:20.

[19]Jubilees 15:31f.; cf. Deuteronomy 32:8f.

[20]Jubilees 23:29.

[21]2 Enoch 29:4f.; cf. 2 Enoch 18 on the story of Genesis 6.

[22]Life of Adam 12-17. For angelic jealousy of man cf. Wisdom of Solomon 2:24; Josephus, Antiquities I.41f.

[23]2 Enoch 31:4.

[24]Ascension of Isaiah 4:2; also 2:4 and 10:29 and cf. Sibylline Oracles III.63.

[25]1 QM 13.4f., 11f. The manuscript evidence favors Beliar in 2 Corinthians 6:15, but other spellings, including Belial, are attested.

[26]Tobit 3:8; 6:13f.

[27]Tobit 6:7.

[28]Tobit 6:15-17.

[29]Tobit 8:3; cf. 3:17 on Raphael given the power "to bind Asmodeus the evil demon."

[30]Testament of Reuben 2.

[31]Testament of Benjamin 3:3f.

[32]Testament of Simeon 3:15; cf. James 4:7.

[33]Testament of Asher 6:5.

[34]1 Enoch 53:3; 56:1; 62:11; 63:1; 66:1.

[35] 1 QS 3.15-4.24. Translation from A. Dupont-Sommer, The Essene Writings from Qumran (Cleveland: World Publishing Co., 1962), pp. 78-82.

[36] CD 16:4f.

[37] Trevor Ling, The Significance of Satan (London: SPCK, 1961), chapter 1.

[38] 1 Enoch 55:4; cf. 90:20-27 on the seventy rulers of the nations ("shepherds") cast into the fiery abyss.

[39] Testament of Zebulun 9:8.

[40] Testament of Simeon 6:6.

[41] Testament of Levi 18:10-12.

[42] Assumption of Moses 10:1.

[43] Philo, Every Good Man is Free 130. Quotations from Philo and Josephus follow the Loeb Classical Library.

[44] Ibid. 39.

[45] Philo, Life of Moses I.276.

[46] Philo, Embassy to Gaius 112; Decalogue 54.

[47] Philo, On the Eternity of the World 64.

[48] Ibid. 76.

[49] Philo, Against Flaccus 168.

[50] Ibid. 179.

[51] Philo, On the Eternity of the World 47.

[52] Philo, Embassy to Gaius 65.

[53] Philo, Noah's Work as a Planter IV.14; On the Giants III.12f. elaborates this. Cf.

Apuleius, The God of Socrates; Plutarch, Obsolescence of Oracles 10 (Moralia 415B-C).

[54]Philo, On the Giants II.6; an almost identical statement in On Dreams I.141. Behind Philo's thought is [Plato,] Epinomis, especially 984D-985B.

[55]Cf. Philo, On the Giants XIII.58.

[56]Philo, On the Giants IV.16.

[57]Ibid.

[58]Matthew 25:41; cf. Ascension of Isaiah 2:2 for Satan, his angels, and his powers.

[59]Cf. Origen, Against Celsus VIII.25.

[60]Josephus, War I.69; cf. I.84, "Let heaven cease to mock."

[61]Josephus, Antiquities XVI.76.

[62]Josephus, War I.233.

[63]Josephus, War IV.41.

[64]Josephus, Life 402.

[65]Josephus, War I. 628 and 556.

[66]Josephus, War I.613.

[67]Josephus, Antiquities XIV.291.

[68]Josephus, Antiquities XVI.20.

[69]Josephus, Against Apion II.263.

[70]Josephus, War I.521; 599; 607; Antiquities XIII.317; 415; 416.

[71]Josephus, Antiquities VI. 166; 168; and 211.

[72]Josephus, War VII.185.

[73] Josephus, Antiquities VIII.45.

[74] Ibid. VIII.46-49.

[75] Ginzberg, op. cit., p. 108f., but somewhat overstated.

[76] Aboth 5:6; cf. bPesahim 54a.

[77] Midrash Rabbah, Genesis 7:5, 5d; cf. Sifre Deuteronomy 33:21 (11,16); Targum Jerusalem I to Numbers 22:28. Quotations from the Midrash are taken from Midrash Rabbah, ed. H. Freedman and M. Simon, 10 vols. (London: Soncino Press, 1939).

[78] Midrash Rabbah, Genesis 20:11, 14a and 24:6, 16a. Other references are bErubim 18b and Tanhuma Bereshith 26, 10b.

[79] bSanhedrin 109a.

[80] bHagigah 16a; the same report in Aboth de Rabbi Nathan 37, 9a. Quotations from the Talmud are taken from the English translation ed. I. Epstein, The Babylonian Talmud, 18 vols. (London: Soncino Press, 1935-1948).

[81] bBerakoth 6a.

[82] Aboth de Rabbi Nathan 37, 9a. Cf. Pesikta Rabbati 6:5: "As He created His world, He created both men and demons in it: the demons see men, but men do not see the demons. He created demons and ministering angels: the ministering angels see the demons, but the demons do not see the ministering angels. He created ministering angels, demons, and men: He sees them all, but no creature can see Him." Translation by William G. Braude, Pesikta Rabbati, 2 vols. (New Haven: Yale, 1968).

[83] bYebamoth 122a.

[84] bYoma 75a.

[85]bBerakoth 6a.

[86]Cf. also Midrash on Psalms 17:8 (65b).

[87]bBerakoth 3a-b; Targum Jerusalem I to Deuteronomy 32:10.

[88]bSanhedrin 65b; bBerakoth 62a; 60b; bShabbath 67a; bPesahim 111b; bYoma 77b; bKiddushin 72a.

[89]bHullin 105b-106a; cf. bPesahim 112a; Midrash on Psalms 20:7.

[90]bShabbath 151b.

[91]bSanhedrin 44a=bMegillah 3a; cf. bPesahim 112b.

[92]bBerakoth 54b.

[93]bBerakoth 43b.

[94]bYoma 21a.

[95]bPesahim 112b.

[96]For the midday demon see bPesahim 111b. Midrash Rabbah, Numbers 12:3 refers to "demons who hold sway at night" and to a midday demon.

[97]Midrash Rabbah, Numbers 14:3 (177c); Pesikta Rabbati 6:7.

[98]Sirach 39:28-31; bBerakoth 54b; Sifre Deuteronomy 32:17, 318 (136b) and 32:24, 321 (137b).

[99]bErubin 41b; bSota 3a, "Resh Lakish said: A person does not commit a transgression unless a spirit of folly enters into him."

[100]bPesahim 112b; bHullin 105b; bYoma 83b; bGittin 67b; Midrash on Psalms 91:3 refers to a man who saw a demon, fell flat, and became epileptic.

[101] Midrash Rabbah, Numbers 19:8.

[102] bHullin 105b.

[103] bPesahim 110a.

[104] bBerakoth 55b.

[105] "Once a demon has looked upon a man, the man sickens and dies"--Midrash on Psalms 17:8 (66a) [English translation by William G. Braude, The Midrash on Psalms, 2 Vols. (New Haven: Yale, 1959)]; cf. 55:3 (146b); Midrash Rabbah Deuteronomy 4:4; cf. bSanhedrin 52a on the "Prince of Gehenna."

[106] bMegillah 11b. The Testament of Solomon develops the theme of Solomon's magical power over demons; see the valuable introduction and translation by D. C. Duling in The Old Testament Pseudepigrapha, ed. James H. Charlesworth, Vol.1 (Garden City: Doubleday, 1983), pp. 935-987.

[107] Pesikta Rabbati 69a; cf. Midrash Rabbah, Exodus 30:16.

[108] bGittin 68a; see also bSotah 48b; Midrash on Psalms 78:12; Midrash Rabbah, Exodus 52:4; Pesikta Rabbati 6:7.

[109] bBaba Bathra 134a; cf. also bKiddushin 29b.

[110] bSanhedrin 65b.

[111] bSanhedrin 101a.

[112] bSanhedrin 67b.

[113] bSanhedrin 65a=bKerioth 3b, which refers to the "prince of demons."

[114] bShabbath 67a.

[115] bShabbath 61a.

[116]bHullin 105b.

[117]bShabbath 104a.

[118]Pesikta Rabbati 5:10; Midrash Rabbah, Numbers 12:3, 4.

[119]Midrash on Psalms 104:24 (224a), "Were it not for the shadow of the Holy One, blessed be He, which protects a man, the demons would destroy him . . . . Were it not for the ordinance of the Holy One . . . ."

[120]Midrash on Psalms 17:8 (65b); 91:4 (199b); Midrash Rabbah, Numbers 12:3.

[121]Midrash on Psalms 104:24 (224a); bShebuoth 15b.

[122]Deuteronomy 6:4-9; 11:3-21; Numbers 15:36-41.

[123]bBerakoth 5a; cf. Midrash Rabbah, Numbers 20:20.

[124]Midrash Rabbah, Numbers 12:3. Cf. the Christian use of the name of Jesus.

[125]bSotah 21a, "Every observance of the Law is a protection." Cf. Midrash on Psalms 91:4 (199a)=Midrash Rabbah, Numbers 12:3.

[126]bKiddushin 29b.

CHAPTER IV

EARLY CHRISTIAN VIEWS ON DEMONOLOGY

Justin, who earned the title Martyr, was a representative Christian teacher and writer in the mid-second century. He gave expression to common views among Christians in the following passage:

> But if this idea take possession of some one, that if we acknowledge God as our helper, we should not, as we say, be oppressed and persecuted by the wicked; this, too, I will solve. God, when he had made the whole world, and subjected things earthly to man, and arranged the heavenly elements for the increase of fruits and rotation of the seasons, and appointed this divine law--for these things also he evidently made for man--committed the care of men and of all things under heaven to angels whom he appointed over them. But the angels transgressed this appointment, and were captivated by love of women, and begat children who are those that are called demons; and besides, they afterwards subdued the human race to themselves, partly by magical writings, and partly by fears and the punishments they occasioned, and partly by teaching them to offer sacrifices, and incense, and libations, of which things they stood in need after they were enslaved by lustful passions; and among men they sowed murders, wars, adulteries, intemperate deeds, and all wickedness. Whence also the poets and mythologists, not knowing that it was the angels and those demons who had been begotten by them that did these things to men, and women, and cities, and nations, which they related, ascribed them to god himself, and to those who were accounted to be his very offspring, and to the offspring of those who were called his brothers, Neptune and Pluto, and

> to the children again of these their off-
> spring. For whatever name each of the
> angels had given himself and his children,
> by that name they called them.

After speaking of God and his Son, Justin
continues:

> For the Son was made man also, having
> been conceived according to the will of
> God the Father, for the sake of believing
> men, and for the destruction of the demons.
> And now you can learn this from what is
> under your own observation. For numberless
> demoniacs throughout the whole world, and
> in your city, many of our Christian men
> exorcising them in the name of Jesus Christ,
> who was crucified under Pontius Pilate,
> have healed and do heal, rendering helpless
> and driving the possessing demons out of
> the men, though they could not be cured by
> all the other exorcists, and those who used
> incantations and drugs.[1]

This passage may serve not only to introduce but
also to outline much that is to be said about
early Christian demonology.[2] Justin speaks concerning the origin of demons (and what that says
about their nature), their involvement in pagan
religion (including its mythology, magic, and
sacrificial rituals), their responsibility for
evils among mankind (including the persecution
of Christians), and the victory of Christ and
Christians over them (including Christian
success in exorcism).

Origin of Demons

Justin refers to the view on the origin of
demons which was expressed in Jewish pseudepigraphal literature of the intertestamental

period: "Angels . . . were captivated by love
of women, and begat children who are those that
are called demons."   According to this view the
"sons of God" in Genesis 6 were angels who came
down and had intercourse with the "daughters of
men."   This interpretation was encouraged by
some manuscripts of the Greek Old Testament
which read "angels of God" in Genesis 6:2.
Moreover, the indebtedness of some early
Christian writers to Jewish speculations in the
pseudepigrapha is greater than is often recognized.[3]   Other Christian authors share Justin's
interpretation that the angels loved virgins
and begot the giants from them and that the souls
of these giants were the demons who wandered
about the world.[4]

Not everyone, however, accepted this view.
Origen, the great biblical scholar and Christian
philosopher from Alexandria, pointed to the book
of 1 Enoch as the source for this view and noted
that 1 Enoch was not scripture in the church.
He was not sure of the meaning of Genesis 6:2
but referred to the interpretation of the story
as an allegory about souls desiring corporal
existence.[5]

Some Christians referred to the idea which
is also found in Jewish sources that the fall of
Satan and his angels was due to envy of Adam as
made in the image of God.   Thus Irenaeus at the
end of the second century said that Satan
because of envy deceived man.[6]   Even Justin says

the devil fell because he deceived Eve.[7] We
also find fairly early in Christian thought a
connection between Isaiah 14:12-15 about the
king of Babylon and Ezekiel 28:1-19 about the
king of Tyre and the fall of Satan.[8] The
earliest uses of these passages would seem to
be that what is said about these kings is an
even truer description of the devil; but this
distinction was soon lost or at least not noted,
and the passages were applied directly to the
fall of Satan.[9]

There was no uniformity in Christian
thought, therefore, about when, where, and why
the demons became rebellious against God; just
as there was no agreement on this in Jewish
thought. By way of contrast, there was consistent testimony to the idea that Satan and the
demons were creatures made by God, who were
created good, and then of their free will
rebelled against God. Origen stated the view
in a memorable way:

> According to our belief, it is true of
> all demons that they were not demons
> originally, but they became so in departing
> from the true way; so that the name "demons"
> is given to those beings who have fallen
> away from God. Accordingly those who
> worship God must not serve demons.[10]

This statement agrees with Origen's declaration,
which agrees with our surviving evidence, that
the "demons" are always bad in Christian usage.[11]
Christian usage thus differed from that of the

Greeks, for whom demons might be good or bad.
Christians used "angels" for good spiritual
beings, although at times this word could be
used of evil beings (as in Matthew 25:11).

Justin once reflected the Greek view that
demons were the souls of the deceased,[12] but his
pupil Tatian denied this.[13] I have noticed
students do not always agree with their
teachers.

Demons, on the early Christian view, were
creatures of God, but not so far as respects
their demoniacal nature; they were made as
rational beings, and then used this improperly.[14]
All spiritual beings were made for perfect sin-
lessness, but some changed into wicked enmity.[15]
"From certain angels, who fell of their own free
will, there sprang a more wicked demon-brood."[16]
Free will was important in early Christian doctrine, and the parallel between human and
angelic free will was explicitly drawn.
Tertullian affirmed that the devil was created
with free will no less than man, and this free
will was operative in man's salvation as well as
in his sin. Man could freely choose the offer
of salvation, even as he had voluntarily chosen
to obey the devil:

> For God afforded room for a conflict,
> wherein man might crush his enemy with the
> same freedom of his will as had made him
> succumb to him (proving that the fault was
> all his own, not God's), and so worthily
> recover his salvation by a victory; where-
> in also the devil might receive a more

bitter punishment, through being vanquished
by him whom he had previously injured.[17]

Given the biblical teaching that there is
only one God, creator of all that exists, and
given the existence of sin, the only conclusion
possible was that Satan and his angels were
creatures of God who had fallen away from his
will. Also, given the silence of scripture on
the origin of the demons, it is no wonder that
speculations assigned different occasions for
the fall.

As fallen angels, the demons were considered to have the same spiritual nature as
angels. They are bodyless.[18] For some writers
this spiritual nature was nonetheless conceived
in a rather material sense, for they considered
spirit to be somewhat material, although assur-
edly a finer grade of matter than can be
perceived. Thus Tatian says demons have received
their structure from matter, but he then elaborates that their structure is spirit, like fire
or air.[19] Only those in whom the Spirit of God
dwells can see them easily. Demons do not partake of flesh, so they do not die like men, but
neither will they partake of everlasting life.[20]
Even a writer like Clement of Alexandria, who
thinks of spirit in non-material terms, sees
their nature as mixed up with other characteristics:

> How then can shades and demons be still
> reckoned gods, being in reality unclean

and impure spirits, acknowledged by all to
be of an earthly and watery nature, sink-
ing downward by their own weight and
flitting about graves and tombs, about
which they appear dimly, being but shadowy
phantasms?[21]

As this passage indicates, the nature of
demons says something about their abode. They
have been cast down from heaven.[22] Most frequently expressed, as was found in Greek and
Jewish thought also, was a dwelling in the
air.[23] But it is also expressed that they haunt
the air and the earth[24] or that water was their
special element.[25]

Pagan Religion

An important kind of Christian literature
in the second and third centuries was the
apology, a defence of Christianity to the pagan
authorities and populace. Justin was one of the
foremost of the Christian apologists. He and
others picked up the suggestions of certain
pagan philosophers that the main features of
pagan religion were due to the demons.[26] The
Christian writers took the idea further and
turned it to their own purposes by giving their
own meaning to demons. The demonic origin of
pagan religion is a pervasive theme in the
writings of the defenders of Christianity. The
demons according to Justin's statement "subdued
the human race to themselves . . . by teaching
them to offer sacrifices, and incense, and
libations, of which things they stood in need . .

. . The poets and mythologists . . . ascribed [these things] to god himself."

Christians followed the lead of the Greek translation of Psalms 96:5 and Jewish thought in identifying the gods of paganism with demons. "We hold," the Christian spokesman Origen said, "that the worship which is supposed among the Greeks to be rendered to gods at the altars, and images, and temples is in reality offered to demons."[27] Justin explained that men "not knowing that these were demons, called them gods, and gave to each the name which each of the demons chose for himself."[28] Tertullian made reference to Paul's words in 1 Corinthians 8:4 that "an idol has no existence" and went on to explain that "the homage" which pagans "render is to demons, who are the real occupants of these consecrated images, whether of dead men or (as they think) of gods."[29] It was charged that demons inspired the mythology on which Greco-Roman paganism rested, especially the immoralities of the deities described in Greek epics.[30]

Minucius Felix, a Latin author of the late second or early third century, has one of the more comprehensive statements about demonic involvement in pagan religion. We will summarize it briefly.[31] The demons are behind the practice of magic. They lurk beside statues and images. They are responsible for the various kinds of divination in pagan religion: they

speak through prophets, control the flight of
birds, direct the lot, control the oracles, etc.
They call men from the true God to material
things. They creep into human bodies and cause
disease and alarm the mind; then they appear to
cure what they have caused. They constrain men
to worship them because they need the fumes and
animals of sacrifice. But they fly from the
presence of Christians. According to Minucius
Felix, then, demons are involved in magic,
idolatry, divination, oracles, healing cults,
and sacrifice.

The words of Minucius Felix may be expanded
and illustrated from the writings of the other
apologists. Thus the incantations and magical
arts common in the ancient world were understood
as invoking demons.[32] Magic, astrology, and
wonders of various kinds were put in the same
category and attributed to the demons.

> These [demons] were the inventors of
> astrology, and soothsaying, and divination,
> and those productions which are called
> oracles, and necromancy, and the art of
> magic, and whatever evil practices besides
> these men exercise, either openly or in
> secret.[33]

Demons were also said to give oracles and enable
persons to foretell the future.[34] The demons
appeared to cure diseases at the healing
sanctuaries, and might cure those which they
themselves caused; but one writer cautioned,
"The demons do not cure, but by their art make
men their captive."[35]

Christians were, of course, opposed to all these features of pagan belief, but it is notable that the typical approach was not to deny that sometimes correct prophecies were spoken, miracles worked, cures effected, or signs given. Rather than becoming involved in these discussions of fact, Christian apologists chose to make their argument on the level of interpretation. Since Christians accepted the supernatural and the possibility of the miraculous, instead of denying that such things could occur, they chose to attribute them to demonic beings. The source and not particular occurrences was the issue. Christians indeed did not grant that all of the wonders told among the pagans actually occurred, but the point is that their case did not rest on whether any given wonder did in fact occur; the Christian case had to do with the source or cause: was it from God and his Spirit or from the devil and his demons? As part of the Christian answer, the argument was made that the moral superiority of Christ and Christianity proved their miracles were from God and not from other powers.[36]

Much of the Christian polemic against paganism had to do with animal sacrifice. Here Christians made the most of certain strands in Hellenistic philosophy which had distinguished the pure spiritual worship of the supreme God from material sacrifice offered to the intermediary demons.[37] Christians made animal

sacrifice really a gross or crude practice.
Athenagoras, who was a sophisticated and philosophically informed apologist of the second
century, graphically stated:

> They who draw men to idols, then, are
> the demons, who are eager for the blood
> of the sacrifices and lick them.

He continues in a statement which shows the
objective acceptance of the activity of demons
and that they find a cooperative attitude in
human minds:

> The demons who hover about matter,
> greedy of sacrificial odors and the blood
> of victims, and ever ready to lead men
> into error, avail themselves of these
> delusive movements of the soul; and taking
> possession of their thoughts cause to flow
> into the mind empty visions as if coming
> from the idols.[38]

The demons actually had need of "sacrifices,
incense, and libations."[39] If they are to remain in the gross air near the earth, they need
food from sacrifice and so keep where there is
always smoke and blood and incense."[40] This was
what made participation in idol sacrifice so
serious for the Christian: although the idol
was nothing, to participate in the sacrifice was
actually to nourish demons.[41]

Demons the Cause of Evils

Justin said, "Among men they sowed murders,
wars, adulteries, intemperate deeds, and all
wickedness."

Tertullian was a learned and skilled

rhetorician in Carthage in North Africa. He
wrote his Apology for Christianity about the
year 200. In that work he included an extended
discussion of demons which is of comparable
significance for early Christian views on demonology to the passage from Justin Martyr with
which we began. He places pagan religion among
the evils which demons cause, but he puts this
in the context of other evils which they cause.
I quote some excerpts:

> We are instructed, moreover, by our
> sacred books how from certain angels, who
> fell of their own free will, there sprang
> a more wicked demon brood, condemned of God
> along with the authors of their race, and
> their chief [Satan]. It will for the pre-
> sent be enough, however, that some account
> is given of their work. Their great
> business is the ruin of mankind. So from
> the very first, spiritual wickedness sought
> our destruction. They inflict, accordingly,
> upon our bodies diseases and other grievous
> calamities, while by violent assaults they
> hurry the soul into sudden and extra-
> ordinary excesses. . . . Demons and angels
> breathe into the soul, and rouse up its
> corruptions with furious passions and vile
> excesses; or with cruel lusts accompanied
> by various errors, of which the worst is
> that by which these deities are commended
> to the favor of deceived and deluded human
> beings, that they may get their proper food
> of flesh-fumes and blood when it is offered
> up to idol images. What is daintier food
> to the spirit of evil, than turning men's
> minds away from the true God by the illu-
> sions of a false divination? And here I
> explain how these illusions are managed.
> Every spirit is possessed of wings. This
> is a common property of both angels and

demons. So they are everywhere in a
single moment; the whole world is as one
place to them; all that is done over the
whole extent of it, it is as easy for them
to know as to report. Their swiftness of
motion is taken for divinity, because their
nature is unknown. Thus they would have
themselves thought sometimes the authors
of the things which they announce; and
sometimes, no doubt, the bad things are
their doing, never the good. . . . Very
kind too, no doubt, they are in regard to
the healing of diseases. For, first of
all, they make you ill; then to get a
miracle out of it, they command the
application of remedies either altogether
new, or contrary to those in use, and
straightway withdrawing hurtful influence,
they are supposed to have wrought a cure.[42]

Demons were blamed by Christian thinkers
for the physical evils in the world. Tertullian
referred to diseases and illnesses which they
cause, and then seem to cure. He illustrated
their effects upon bodies and souls by the way
an unseen poison in the breeze can blight crops.
Other writers explicitly included blight and
crop failures among the natural disasters caused
by demons. To the evil spirits "belong famine,
blasting of the vine and fruit trees, pestilence
among men and beasts; all these are the proper
occupations of demons."[43] "Wicked spirits are
the cause of plagues, barrenness, tempests, or
other calamities."[44]

The main work of demons, however, was seen
in the moral sphere. Or, at least, more attention was given to their activity in relation to

human beings. They do ill to mankind.[45] The
demons try to keep men from God,[46] "inciting
and instigating men to sin."[47] The demon chief
had been deceiving mankind in order to lead them
away from God since the beginning. With reference to Genesis 3 one author spoke of "the
misanthropic demon" who deceived Adam and Eve
into thinking that there were gods in addition
to the One God and so they too could become gods.
"Men, therefore, having been duped by the deceiving demon, and having dared to disobey God,
were cast out of Paradise."[48] The identification of the serpent with a demon, Satan, and
the dragon was usual.[49] To deceive is still
Satan's work, but this is also the limit of what
he can do:

> The devil, however, as he is the
> apostate angel, can only go to this length,
> as he did at the beginning, to deceive and
> lead astray the mind of man into disobeying
> the commandments of God, and gradually to
> darken the hearts . . . .[50]

The theme of the devil's and demons' deceptive-
ness recurs continually.[51] And this is
particularly associated with leading their
followers into sin.[52]

So close was the association of temptation
and sin with the work of demons that various
evil impulses and acts could themselves be called
demons. For instance, the early Christian pro-
phet Hermas says "evil speaking is a restless
demon,"[53] and again, "presumption and vain

confidence is a great demon."[54] This identification was similar to the way in which the
Jewish work The Testaments of the Twelve
Patriarchs spoke of evil desires. Hermas is
also close to the language of the Dead Sea
Scrolls in assigning an angel of righteousness
and an angel of wickedness to each person.[55]
Origen later declared that the malignant power
suggests evil and the divine power suggests good
to each person, but we have freedom of will in
regard to both.[56] The identification of sinful
impulses with demons was much developed in early
monastic literature. Human passions were objec-
tified and personified as demons, even to the
point of being visualized. When the devil suggested foul thoughts to the hermit Antony, the
latter countered them with prayers. "And the
devil one night even took upon him the shape of
a woman and imitated all her movements simply to
beguile Antony."[57]

Demonic temptations to sin were not considered to overpower human beings. As indicated
by the statement of Origen above, free will was
preserved. The emphasis on free will was consistently maintained in the early fathers.[58]
The demons were simply seen as the source of the
sin. But they found their opportunity from the
inclination of human beings toward sin. The
demons "take as their ally the desire which by
nature is in each person for every different
kind of evil."[59] They "subdue all who do not

struggle against them on behalf of their own salvation."[60] "For the demons, inspired with frenzy against men by reason of their own wickedness, pervert their minds, which already incline downwards . . . that they may be disabled from rising to the path that leads to heaven."[61] Origen explained that the "occasions of stumbling" in Matthew 18:7 are "an army of the devil, his angels, and a wicked band of impure spirits, which seeking out instruments through whom they will work, often find men altogether strangers to piety, and sometimes even some of those who are thought to believe the Word of God."[62] The power of demons over human life, therefore, comes from men's choice not to follow God. The demons "have been set by the Word, who governs all things, to rule over those who subjected themselves to evil and not to God."[63] Some writers also explicitly recognized the influence of environment. Thus Tertullian spoke of demons surrounding those born into heathen homes from their birth,[64] an influence from which Christian homes were spared; but he explained that this was not the only cause of sin, for there is an impurity in our nature. Origen noted that some Christians blamed their sins on demons, but he explained that in addition to sins to which demons tempt us, there are those which we originate; but in either case our will cooperates.[65] Demons have no power unless one of his own accord gives himself over to them.[66]

Since the demons were, even in their rebellious state, still creatures of God, they must ultimately serve his will. So, Origen sees the things which they bring on mankind serving useful functions:

> In the capacity of public executioners the demons receive power at certain times to carry out the divine judgments, for the restoration of those who have plunged headlong into wickedness, or for the trial and discipline of the souls of the wise.[67]

Demonic activity was directed especially against those who tried to be faithful to God. The demons were seen as "warring and fighting most keenly against the salvation of those who devote themselves to God."[68] A principal expression of this demonic opposition to God was the persecution of Christians by the Roman Empire. That the demons were to blame for the persecutions is frequently stated.[69] To make the demons responsible for persecution was perhaps an apologetic ploy to avoid placing the blame directly on the State; on the other hand, to say that the rulers were the tools of demons was not particularly complimentary, and so this view may be taken as genuinely believed. The rulers and magistrates were excused to an extent. They opposed Christianity, according to the apologists, because they had been deceived by the demons.[70] They were still culpable, and the apologists tried hard to remove the deception. Although the demons stirred up the persecutions,

the apologists expressed the confidence that
they could not accomplish the destruction of
Christians and pointed out that the word of God
advanced in spite of opposition.[71]

Another expression of demonic opposition
to Christianity was to raise up false teachers
to lead men away from the truth.[72] But neither
attack from without nor error from within could
overcome God's church and God's truth. Even
these things fit into God's providential design
according to Tertullian:

> We believe that persecution comes to
> pass, no question, by the devil's agency,
> but not by the devil's origination. Satan
> will not be at liberty to do anything
> against the servants of the living God
> unless the Lord grant leave, either that he
> may overthrow Satan himself by the faith of
> the elect which proves victorious in the
> trial, or in the face of the world show
> that apostatizers to the devil's cause have
> been in reality his servants.[73]

Christians by their steadfastness and faith con-
tributed to the overthrow of Satan. Not all may
have chosen to allow that the persecution was by
God's leave, but they would have shared
Tertullian's conviction that ultimately God was
in control. There was a reason for the Christian
confidence in the face of a hostile world.

Victory of Christ and Christians

As Justin Martyr said in our opening
quotation, Christ "was made man . . . for the
destruction of the demons." Christian confidence in the face of persecution, temptation,

sin, and all the evils in the world was due to belief in the victory of Christ over the demonic powers.

The incarnation itself was seen as, if not accomplishing, at least initiating, the overthrow of the demons. The evil demon was "overcome by Christ as soon as he was born."[74] Christ submitted to become flesh and be born of the virgin of the family of David in order that the serpent who sinned from the beginning and the angels like him might be destroyed.[75] The evil spirits became feeble and lost strength at the birth of Jesus.[76] At his temptation Jesus "destroyed and overthrew the devil."[77] His baptism was another time when he defeated the demons, thought of as dwelling in the waters, a symbol of death: "Since, therefore, it was necessary to break the heads of the dragon in pieces, he went down and bound the strong one in the waters."[78] Jesus' ministry also accomplished the defeat of the demons. He "put to flight multitudes of demons" when he went about healing and delivering men.[79]

The crucifixion of Jesus was preeminently the moment of the defeat of Satan. "The concealed power of God was in Christ the crucified, before whom demons, and all the principalities and powers of the earth, tremble."[80] It was "through Jesus, who was crucified," that "the demons would be destroyed, and would dread his name, and that all principalities and kingdoms

would fear him."[81] Succinctly stated, by the
"cross Satan and every opposing power was routed
and triumphed over."[82] Irenaeus, bishop of
Lyons in Gaul in the late second century, took
the idea of Christ's victory over the devil as
the key motif in developing his doctrine of the
atonement. Irenaeus applied Jesus' parable of
binding the strong man in Matthew 12:29 and
Luke 11:21f. to the coming of Jesus and as ex-
plaining the significance of Jesus' victory over
Satan. Jesus' total obedience to the will of
the Father reversed the effects of the transgression of Adam. As Satan had made mankind his
captives by sin, Christ now made Satan captive
through his obedience.[83]

The final overthrow and punishment of the
demons, however, must await the second coming of
Christ. The demons attempt to escape the power
of Christ.[84] After the resurrection Christ was
taken to heaven to await the consummation, that
is "until he has subdued his enemies the
demons."[85] When he comes again, he will send
the wicked "into everlasting fire with the
wicked demons."[86]

In the interval between the first and
second coming of Christ, the preaching of the
gospel is a means of the defeat of the demons.
The message of Christ, when it is believed and
obeyed, brings about the overthrow of evil.
"His mighty word has persuaded many to abandon
the demons whom they formerly served and through

it to believe on the almighty God."[87] "After
being persuaded by the Word, we keep away from
demons."[88] The heart of that message is the
cross. Through its power, "some out of all the
nations . . . have turned from vain idols and
demons to serve God."[89] One explanation offered
for the intense opposition of the demons to
Christianity was that they saw the libations and
odors in which they delighted being swept away
by the prevalence of the instructions of Jesus.
But God who sent Jesus dissipated all the con-
spiracies of the demons and made the gospel
prevail.[90]

By reason of the victory won by Christ, or
at least initiated and assured by his death and
resurrection, Christians could have confidence
that they would prevail over the demons. By
reason of his baptism, the Christian had been
delivered from the power of demons and had been
identified with Christ. In an imaginative comparison with Israel's escape from the armies of
Egypt at the Red Sea, Christians were described
as escaping from the demons whose presence and
influence were drowned in the waters of baptism.

> Paul calls that crossing conferred in
> the cloud and the sea a baptism [1 Corinth-
> ians 10:1-4] in order to bring home to you
> who were baptized in Christ, in water and
> the Holy Spirit, that the Egyptians are
> pursuing you, striving to subject you to
> them, I mean, the "rulers of this world"
> and the "Spirits of wickedness" to whom
> you gave your allegiance. They strive to

follow you, while you go down into the
water, where you are safe, and when you
have been purified from all stain of sin,
come forth a new man, to sing the new
song.[91]

As another writer put it, the old tyrant,
Pharaoh, pursued Israel even to the sea; and now
the devil follows us to the very streams of
salvation. "The tyrant of old was drowned in
the sea; and this present one disappears in the
water of salvation."[92] The early Christian baptismal ceremony came to include various ritual
exorcisms in order to dramatize the driving
away of demons and deliverance into the realm
of Christ.[93] But these were not as effective as
baptism:

> The obstinate wickedness of the devil
> prevails even up to the saving water, but
> in baptism it loses all the poison of his
> wickedness. An instance of this we see in
> the king Pharaoh, who, having struggled
> long, and delayed in his perfidy, could
> resist and prevail until he came to the
> water; but when he had come thither, he
> was both conquered and destroyed. [There
> follows 1 Corinthians 10:1-6.] And this
> also is done in the present day, in that
> the devil is scourged, and burned, and
> tortured by exorcists, by the human voice
> and by divine power; and although he often
> says that he is going out, and will leave
> the men of God, yet in that which he says
> he deceives, and puts in practice what was
> before done by Pharaoh with the same
> obstinate and fraudulent deceit. When,
> however, they come to the water of sal-
> vation and to the sanctification of baptism,
> we ought to know and to trust that there
> the devil is beaten down, and the man,
> dedicated to God, is set free by the divine

> mercy. For as scorpions and serpents,
> which prevail on the dry ground, when cast
> into water, cannot prevail nor retain
> their venom; so also the wicked spirits,
> which are called scorpions and serpents,
> and yet are trodden under foot by us, by
> the power given by the Lord, cannot remain
> any longer in the body of a man in whom,
> baptized and sanctified, the Holy Spirit is
> beginning to dwell.[94]

One gains the definite impression that for many early Christians more important than the promise of forgiveness of sins was the promise of deliverance from demons.[95]

One of the earliest Christian writers after the New Testament stated that "Before we believed in God our heart [was a temple of idolatry,] a house of demons through doing things contrary to God," but now they are a temple of God.[96] Origen declared, "We do not, then, deny that there are many demons upon earth, but we maintain that they exist and exercise power among the wicked, as a punishment of their wickedness. But they have no power over those who 'Put on the whole armor of God' [Ephesians 6:11]."[97] "The Christian--the true Christian, I mean--who has submitted to God alone and his Word, will suffer nothing from demons, for He is mightier than demons. . . . For we despise them, and the demons, when despised, can do no harm to those who are under the protection of Him who can alone help all who deserve his aid."[98] "And Christians have nothing to fear, even if demons should not be well-disposed to

them; for they are protected by the Supreme God
. . . . [The Christian] may say with confidence
that he has nothing to suffer from the whole
host of demons."[99] Origen further connected the
success of individual Christians in banishing
demons from their lives with the general decline
of demonic influence in the world and the expansion of Christianity.

> Anyone who vanquishes a demon in him-
> self, e.g. the demon of lewdness, puts it
> out of action; the demon is cast into the
> abyss, and cannot do any harm to anyone.
> Hence there are far fewer demons now than
> before; hence, also, a large number of
> demons having been overthrown, the heathen
> are now free to believe, as they would not
> be did whole legions of demons exist as
> formerly.[100]

The Christian, of course, must be faithful
to God and claim the divine aid available to
him. To continue in prayer is prominent in the
instructions given to Christians concerning what
will keep them from the deceitful demons and
enable them to remain blameless.[101] Prayer
enables Christians to resist the evil spirit.[102]

Persecution, as noted above, was viewed as
inspired by the demons. The demonic assault on
Christianity meant that some Christians would
have to face martyrdom. And martyrdom was seen
as a direct confrontation with the devil. One
of the courageous female martyrs of the early
church, Perpetua, in her diary recorded: "I
realized that it was not with wild animals that
I would fight but with the Devil, but I knew

that I would win the contest."[103]   As demons
caused the persecution, so martyrdom was a
struggle against them.[104]   The martyr was called
upon to share in the death of Christ.   Just as
Christ conquered the demons by dying, so
Christians overcame them by dying for their
faith in Christ.   So, it is frequently affirmed
that the demons were defeated and overpowered by
the martyrs for the truth.[105]

I am persuaded that an important factor in
the Christian success in the Roman world was the
promise which it made of deliverance from
demons.   Greco-Roman paganism was quite demon-
conscious, as seen in our second chapter.   A
religion which offered victory over the demonic
would have had a powerful appeal--especially, if
that religion could offer convincing evidence of
its power over demons.   The courage and confidence of the martyrs was one such demonstration.
Another was seen in the practice of casting out
demons from those who were possessed.

Exorcism

Although demons had influence only over
those who freely allowed them to be in control,
it was thought possible for one to come completely or largely under the power of a demon.
On the other hand, the victory that Christ had
won gave to his followers, in his name, a power
over the evil spirits.   Early Christian literature is full of references to the power of
Christians to expel demons in the name of

Christt.[106]   As Justin said, "Numberless
demoniacs throughout the whole world . . . many
of our Christian men . . . have healed."   Justin
indeed made much in his apologetic for
Christianity of the ability of Christians to
exorcise demons. That this was done "in the
name of Jesus Christ" was taken as a proof of
the truth and power of Christianity. "And now
we who believe on our Lord Jesus who was crucified under Pontius Pilate exorcise all demons
and evil spirits and have them subject to us."[107]
The power is regularly ascribed to the name of
Jesus Christ, and he is usually further identified as the one "who was crucified under Pontius
Pilate."[108]   Tatian, pupil of Justin, refers to
diseases from natural causes, which demons
ascribed to themselves in order to gain attention from those afflicted, and to afflictions
which they themselves cause: "Sometimes they
themselves disturb the habit of a body by a
tempest of folly; but, being smitten by the word
of God, they depart in terror, and the sick man
is healed."[109]   Tertullian refers to demons
knowing things about spiritual reality which
human beings do not acknowledge. He says to
pagans:

> Mock as you like, but get the demons if
> you can to join you in your mocking; let
> them deny that Christ is coming to judge
> every human soul . . . . Let them deny
> that, for their wickedness condemned
> already, they are kept for that very judg-
> ment day, with all their worshippers and

> their works. Why, all the authority and
> power we have over them is from our naming
> the name of Christ, and recalling to their
> memory the woes with which God threatens
> them. . . . Fearing Christ in God, and
> God in Christ, they become subject to the
> servants of God and Christ. So at our
> touch and breathing, overwhelmed by the
> thought and realization of those judgment
> fires, they leave at our command the bodies
> they have entered, unwilling and dis-
> tressed.[110]

The cure or deliverance might not always be
instantaneous: Minucius Felix says the demons
either leap forth at once or vanish by degrees,
as a result of the faith of the sufferer or the
grace of the healer.[111]

Pagans and Jews had their stories of
exorcism, as seen in the preceding two chapters,
and as Christians well knew. Christians, however, claimed to be more effective. The name of
the Son of God expels every demon, in contrast
to Jewish exorcisms (only sometimes effective)
and to pagan magic.[112] Moreover, Christians
pointed to a difference in manner in which their
exorcists worked. The pagan philosopher Celsus,
who in the second century launched a powerful
literary attack on Christianity, charged that
the Christian exorcisms were done by magical
incantations. Origen in his reply to Celsus
affirmed, "It is not by incantations that
Christians seem to prevail, but by the name of
Jesus, accompanied by the announcement of the
narratives which relate to him."[113]

Elsewhere Origen says that it was by prayers and
other means learned from scripture that demons
were driven out of the souls of men and out of
the bodies of animals, not by magic or incantations.[114]   Origen further tells Christians not
to adjure, question, or speak directly to the
demon, but rather to pray and fast.[115]   The
distinctiveness of Christian exorcism was most
fully put in the following passage:

> This also, again, is suitable and right
> and comely for those who are brethren in
> Christ, that they should visit those who
> are harassed by evil spirits, and pray and
> pronounce adjurations over them, intel-
> ligently, offering such prayer as is
> acceptable before God; not with a multitude
> of fine words, well prepared and arranged,
> so that they may appear to men eloquent
> and of a good memory. Such men are "like
> a sounding pipe, or a tinkling cymbal";
> and they bring no help to those over whom
> they make their adjurations; but they speak
> with terrible words, and affright people,
> but do not act with true faith, according
> to the teaching of our Lord, who hath said:
> "This kind goeth not out but by fasting and
> prayer," offered unceasingly and with
> earnest mind. And let them holily ask and
> beg of God, with cheerfulness and all cir-
> cumspection and purity, without hatred and
> without malice. In this way let us
> approach a brother or sister who is sick,
> and visit them in a way that is right,
> without guile, and without covetousness,
> and without noise, and without talkative-
> ness, and without such behavior as is alien
> from the fear of God, and without haughti-
> ness, but with the meek and lowly spirit of
> Christ. Let them, therefore, with fasting
> and with prayer make their adjurations, and
> not with the elegant and well-arranged and

fitly-ordered words of learning, but as men
who have received the gift of healing from
God, confidently, to the glory of God. By
your fastings and prayers and perpetual
watching, together with your other good
works, mortify the works of the flesh by
the power of the Holy Spirit. He who acts
thus "is a temple of the Holy Spirit of
God." Let this man cast out demons, and
God will help him.116

Conclusion

Christian authors of the second to fourth
centuries reflected the common beliefs of their
time about a host of intermediary beings between God and man. To the views drawn from
their Greco-Roman and Jewish environments they
added distinctively Christian convictions. At
the risk of over simplifying and of minimizing
differences between authors we may summarize
some of the quite generally held views among
early post-New Testament Christians. They accepted the reality of the spiritual world, in which
there are both good angels and wicked demons.
All were creatures of God and originally good.
Some angels in the exercise of their free will,
at some point, rebelled against God and fell
from their heavenly abode. This may have been
a pre-temporal fall, have occurred in connection
with the creation of man, been out of envy, or
have been connected with the sinfulness in the
days of Noah. The demons were responsible for
the physical evils in the world, stood behind
all false religion, induced the persecution of
true religion, and tried to tempt men into

sinning against God. Those who did so were punished by serving the demons. The demons'
spheres of activity, therefore, were the cosmos,
governmental structures, and individuals. But
on all levels their power was ultimately subject
to God. Their defeat had been sealed and assured by the life, ministry, death, and
resurrection of Jesus. At his second coming
the demons and all who followed them would receive punishment. Meanwhile, those who believed
in Jesus and followed the will of God had power
over demons. This was dramatically demonstrated
in the ability of Christians to drive away
demons in the name of Jesus Christ. Wherever
paganism was practiced and human beings gave
themselves to the will of demons, there demonic
influence was felt; but wherever the gospel was
preached and the influence of Christ was felt,
the demons were powerless. However one views
the demons, that seems to be a viewpoint
historically justified.

Notes

[1] *2 Apology* 5. Quotations from early
Christian literature are taken from the *Ante-
Nicene Fathers*, ed. Alexander Roberts and James
Donaldson (reprint at Grand Rapids: William
B. Eerdmans, 1950) and *Nicene* and *Post-Nicene
Fathers*, ed. Philip Schaff and Henry Wace
(reprint at Grand Rapids: William B. Eerdmans,
1952) where available.

[2] For the contents of this chapter, in
addition to the general bibliography see Adolf
Harnack, *The Mission and Expansion of
Christianity* (reprint at New York: Harper,
1961), pp. 125-146; F. X. Gokey, *The Terminology
for the Devil and Evil Spirits in the Apostolic
Fathers* (Washington: Catholic University Press,
1961); H. Wey, *Die Funktionen der bösen Geister
bei den griechischen Apologeten des 2
Jahrhunderten nach Christus* (Winterthur: P. G.
Keller, 1957). There are a number of studies
devoted to the demonology of particular writers:
e.g., E. Ferguson, "The Demons according to
Justin Martyr," *The Man of the Messianic Reign*,
ed. Wil C. Goodheer (Wichita Falls: Western
Christian Foundation, 1980), pp. 103-112; Emil
Scheweiss, *Angels and Demons according to
Lactantius* (Washington: Catholic University
Press, 1944); H. J. Schoeps, "Die Dämonologie der
Pseudoklementinen," *Aus frühchristlicher Zeit*
(Tübingen, 1950), pp. 38-81; A. C. Baynes, "St.
Anthony and the Demons," *Journal of Egyptian
Archaeology* 40(1954), pp. 7-10; Michael P. McHugh,
"The Demonology of Saint Ambrose in Light of the
Tradition," *Wiener Studien* 12(1978), pp. 205-231;
G. J. M. Bartelink, "Le diable et les démons
dans les oeuvres de Jérôme,""*Studia Patristica*
17 (Oxford: Pergamon Press, 1982), pp. 463-469.

[3] Demonstrated in reference to Irenaeus by
D. R. Schultz, "The Origin of Sin in Irenaeus
and Jewish Pseudepigraphical Literature,"
Vigiliae Christianae 32 (1978) 161-190.

[4] E.g. Athenagoras, *Plea* 24-25.

[5] Against Celsus V.54f.

[6] Proof of the Apostolic Preaching 16; cf. Against Heresies IV.40.3; Tertullian, On Patience 5; Gregory of Nyssa, Catechetical Oration 6.

[7] Dialogue with Trypho 124.

[8] Origen, Against Celsus VI.43; On First Principles I.5.5; Tertullian, Against Marcion II.10.

[9] E.g. Cyril of Jerusalem, Catechetical Lectures II.4.

[10] Against Celsus VII.69.

[11] Ibid. VIII.25; 39; V.5; he does use the qualifier "wicked," for instance in VII.69. Cf. Tertullian, Apology 32.

[12] 1 Apology 18.

[13] Address 16.

[14] Origen, Against Celsus IV.65; Irenaeus, Against Heresies IV.41.1f.

[15] Tertullian, Shows 2.

[16] Tertullian, Apology 22.

[17] Tertullian, Against Marcion II.10.

[18] Ignatius, Smyrnaeans 2; 3.

[19] Address 12 and 15.

[20] Ibid. 14.

[21] Exhortation 4. Cf. the descriptions in Plutarch in Chapter II.

[22] Tatian, Address 20.

[23]Tertullian, Apology 22; cf. Ascension of Isaiah 4.1f.

[24]Athenagoras, Plea 25.

[25]Aristides, Apology 4--wind ministers to God, fire to angels, and water to demons. The influence of Psalms 104:4 has altered the philosophical view which associated fire with god, air with demons, water with heroes, and earth with men--Plutarch, The Obsolescence of Oracles 10 (Moralia 415B).

[26]An extensive collection of quotations from pagan philosophers--principally Plutarch and Porphyry--is made by Eusebius in his Preparation for the Gospel V on the connection of demons with pagan religious practices, especially oracles.

[27]Against Celsus VII.69; cf. VII.65. The identification is frequent: e.g. Tatian, Address 8; 29; Theophilus, To Autolycus I.10; Tertullian, To Scapula 2; On Idolatry 1; 15; Acts of John 41; 43; cf. Epistle of Barnabas 16:7. Justin regularly quotes Psalms 96:5 as saying, "the gods of the nations are idols of demons"--1 Apology 41; Dialogue with Trypho 58; 73.

[28]1 Apology 5; cf. 9.

[29]Shows 13.

[30]Justin, 1 Apology 25; 21; Tatian, Address 8; Theophilus, To Autolycus II.8; cf. Plutarch, Obsolescence of Oracles 13-15 and Isis and Osiris 25 and see chapter II.

[31]Octavius 26-27.

[32]Origen, Against Celsus VII.69.

[33]Lactantius, Divine Institutes II.17; cf. Tertullian, Apology 23; 35; On Idolatry 9; Hippolytus, Refutation of All Heresies IV.28; 35.

[34]Origen, Against Celsus IV.93; VII.3 and 6.
Cf. the girl at Philippi with the "spirit of
divination" in Acts 16:16-18 and Pseudo-Clement,
Homilies IX.16.

[35]Tatian, Address 18.

[36]Lactantius, Divine Institutes IV.15 makes
the distinction that God works miracles and
demons work magic. Origen especially makes the
moral argument, as in Against Celsus I.68;
III.28. For the larger issue see E. R. Dodds,
Pagan and Christian in an Age of Anxiety
(Cambridge: University Press, 1965), 124ff.
For the debate between the pagan Celsus and the
Christian Origen on how to classify Jesus, see
Eugene V. Gallagher, Divine Man or Magician:
Celsus and Origen on Jesus (Chico, CA: Scholars
Press, 1982) and for the interpretations magic
or miracle see Harold Remus, "'Magic or
Miracle'? Some Second Century Instances," The
Second Century 2 (1982) pp. 127-156.

[37]Plutarch, Obsolescence of Oracles 13-14;
Celsus in Origen, Against Celsus VIII.60-63;
Porphyry, Abstinence II.42.

[38]Plea 26 and 27.

[39]Justin, 2 Apology 5; cf. 1 Apology 12.

[40]Origen, Exhortation to Martyrdom 45 in
Library of Christian Classics, vol. 2, ed. J. E.
L. Oulton and Henry Chadwick (Philadelphia:
Westminster 1954); cf. Against Celsus VII.35;
VIII.30; 64; IV. 32; III.28.

[41]Origen, Exhortation to Martyrdom 45;
Against Celsus III.37; cf. Tertullian, To
Scapula 2.

[42]Apology 22; cf. Soul's Testimony 3.

[43]Origen, Against Celsus VIII.31.

[44]Ibid. I.31.

[45] Ibid. VIII.36.

[46] Justin, 1 Apology 58; cf. Tertullian, Shows 10.

[47] Origen, On First Principles III.2.1. For the following section note especially Clement of Alexandria, Miscellanies II.20, which uses "spiritual powers," "evil spirits," and "demons" interchangeably.

[48] Pseudo-Justin, Hortatory Address to the Greeks 21.

[49] Theophilus, To Autolycus II.28 employs all four terms together. Cf. Justin, 1 Apology 28; Revelation 12:9.

[50] Irenaeus, Against Heresies V.24.3.

[51] E.g. Justin, 1 Apology 5; 14.

[52] Tatian, Address 14.

[53] Mandates 2:3; cf. Similitudes 9:23:5.

[54] Similitudes 9:23:3.

[55] Mandates 6:2:1ff.; cf. Epistle of Barnabas 18:1f.

[56] On First Principles III.2.4.

[57] Athanasius, Life of Antony 5. At other times the demons took the form of wild animals-- 9; cf. 6; 23; 51.

[58] For instance in Justin, 1 Apology 43; Dialogue with Trypho 102; 141.

[59] Justin, 1 Apology 10; cf. 14.

[60] Justin, 1 Apology 43; cf. Dialogue with Trypho 102; 141.

[61] Tatian, Address 16.

[62] Commentary on Matthew 13:22

[63] Origen, Against Celsus VIII.33.

[64] On the Soul 39.

[65] Origen, On First Principles III.2.1ff.

[66] Pseudo-Clement, Homilies IX.23.

[67] Against Celsus VIII.31.

[68] Ibid. VIII.64.

[69] From Justin Martyr note 1 Apology 5; 57; 2 Apology 1; 7; 8; 12; Dialogue with Trypho 18; 131.

[70] Justin, 1 Apology 10; 14; 2 Apology 13.

[71] Origen, Against Celsus IV.32; cf. Exhortation to Martyrdom 32.

[72] Justin, 1 Apology 26; 56; 58; Hippolytus, Refutation of All Heresies VI.2; cf. VII.20.

[73] Tertullian, On Flight 2.

[74] Justin, Dialogue with Trypho 78.

[75] Ibid. 45.

[76] Origen, Against Celsus I.60.

[77] Justin, Dialogue with Trypho 125; cf. Irenaeus, Against Heresies V.21.1-3.

[78] Cyril of Jerusalem, Catechetical Lectures III.10.

[79] Origen, Against Celsus VIII.64.

[80] Justin, Dialogue with Trypho 49.

[81] Ibid. 131; cf. 30.

[82] Serapion, Prayerbook 16.

[83] Against Heresies V.21.1 and 3; III.23.1.
See Gustaf Aulén, Christus Victor (London: SPCK, 1961), pp. 32-51; H. E. W. Turner, The Patristic Doctrine of Redemption (London, 1952), pp. 47-69; an existential interpretation is given by John Macquarrie, "Demonology and the Classic Idea of Atonement," Expository Times 68(1956), pp. 3-6.

[84] Justin, 1 Apology 40.

[85] Ibid. 45.

[86] Ibid. 52; cf. 2 Apology 7-8.

[87] Justin, Dialogue with Trypho 83.

[88] Justin, 1 Apology 14.

[89] Justin, Dialogue with Trypho 91; cf. 12.

[90] Origen, Against Celsus III.29.

[91] Origen, Homilies on Exodus V.1-2.

[92] Cyril of Jerusalem, Catechetical Lectures XIX.2-3.

[93] E. Ferguson, "Baptismal Motifs in the Ancient Church," Restoration Quarterly 7 (1963) 209-211; ibid., Early Christians Speak (Austin: Sweet Publishing Co., 1971), 39f.

[94] Cyprian, Epistle 75:15.

[95] Pseudo-Clement, Homilies IX.19 says that being baptized "you shall not only be able to drive away the spirits which lurk in you," but also to drive them from others.

[96] Epistle of Barnabas 16:7; cf. Irenaeus, Against Heresies III.8.2.

[97] Origen, Against Celsus VIII.34.

[98] Ibid. VIII.36.

[99] Ibid. VIII.27.

[100] Origen, Homily on Joshua XV.5, quoted in Harnack, op. cit., p. 143.

[101] Justin, Dialogue with Trypho 30.

[102] Origen, On Prayer 12:1; 13:3.

[103] Passion of Perpetua and Felicitas 10.

[104] Tertullian, Apology 27.

[105] Origen, Against Celsus VIII.44; cf. VIII. 64.

[106] For accounts of exorcism see Acts of Peter 11; Acts of Thomas 42-49; 73-81; and cf. the claim of Irenaeus, Against Heresies II.32.4.

[107] Dialogue with Trypho 76.

[108] Ibid. 30; 76; 85; 2 Apology 6 and 8. Theophilus, To Autolycus II.8 speaks of exorcism "in the name of the living and true God."

[109] Address 16.

[110] Tertullian, Apology 23.

[111] Octavius 27.

[112] Justin, Dialogue with Trypho 85. Cf. Origen, Against Celsus I.68 for Celsus' reference to pagan magicians who "expel demons from men"; also VI.39f.

[113] Origen, Against Celsus I.6; cf. VIII.58. See note 36.

[114] Ibid. VII.4; 57. To nuance this claim, see references in chapter I, note 11.

[115] Commentary on Matthew 13:7. For fasting as means of casting out demons, Apocalypse of Elijah iv.8f.

[116] Pseudo-Clement, On Virginity I.12.

CHAPTER V

THE CHRISTIAN STANCE TOWARD THE DEMONIC

> Finally, be strong in the Lord and in
> the strength of his might. Put on the
> whole armor of God, that you may be able
> to stand against the wiles of the devil.
> For we are not contending against flesh
> and blood, but against the principalities,
> against the powers, against the world
> rulers of this present darkness, against
> the spiritual hosts of wickedness in the
> heavenly places. Therefore take the whole
> armor of God, that you may be able to with-
> stand in the evil day, and having done all,
> to stand. Stand therefore, having girded
> your loins with truth, and having put on
> the breastplate of righteousness, and
> having shod your feet with the equipment of
> the gospel of peace; above all taking the
> shield of faith, with which you can quench
> all the flaming darts of the evil one. And
> take the helmet of salvation, and the sword
> of the Spirit, which is the word of God.
> Pray at all times in the Spirit, with all
> prayer and supplication. To that end keep
> alert with all perseverance, making sup-
> plication for all the saints. (Ephesians
> 6:10-18)

This passage seems to me to be the best
description of the Christian stance toward the
demonic. As we come in this final chapter to
consider the Christian's attitude toward the
demonic and what our conduct should be today, we
want to lay a firm biblical foundation.[1] For
that we shall consider the New Testament writings outside the gospels, which we considered in
our first chapter. These writings give us the
post-resurrection position of Christians in the
world. The Pauline literature will be our

143

principal interest for this biblical study, but
we will supplement what Paul says with other
authors, particularly the Johannine writings.

The Pauline corpus uses the word "demons"
in only two contexts, both of which assign functions to demons with which we are familiar from
preceding studies. In 1 Corinthians 10:19-21
Paul follows the usual Jewish interpretation
that idols are nothing, but that the pagan gods
are actually demons:

> What do I imply then? That food offered
> to idols is anything, or that an idol is
> anything? No, I imply that what pagans
> sacrifice they offer to demons and not to
> God. I do not want you to be partners with
> demons. You cannot drink the cup of the
> Lord and the cup of demons. You cannot
> partake of the table of the Lord and the
> table of demons.[2]

Thus does Paul argue against the Christian
participating in pagan religious ceremonies,
particularly eating the sacred meals that were
part of idolatrous worship. The other Pauline
usage of demons is in a more distinctively
Christian context: "Now the Spirit expressly
says that in later times some will depart from
the faith by giving heed to deceitful spirits
and doctrines of demons" (1 Timothy 4:1). We
notice here the equivalence of spirits and demons and the designation of these beings as
"deceitful." Such usage is common enough. Less
common is the indication that heresy, or false
doctrine, is to be attributed to demonic

influence. This was a thought, however, very
frequently picked up by later Christian authors
as they confronted schism and false teaching
among professing Christians. The practices advocated by the false teachers opposed here were
among those advocated by the Gnostics who posed
such a challenge to the church in the second-
century--forbidding marriage and enjoining abstinence from meat, the asceticism which
challenged the goodness of God's creation in the
interests of a false spirituality.

Therefore, Paul did not use the word
"demons" very much. The equivalent in the
Pauline corpus was "principalities and powers,"
as in Ephesians 6, where is added "world rulers
of this present darkness" and "spiritual hosts
of wickedness." The terms "principalities and
powers" were in use in Jewish literature for
angelic beings.[3] Paul seems to apply various
titles to spiritual beings indiscriminately and
to make no effort at a systematic presentation.
"Principalities and powers" may not be identical
with what other writers of the time called
"demons" (but I think would include them); nevertheless the principles stated about them would
apply to demons or any powers and influences that
would challenge the lordship of Christ.

Apart from the Synoptic Gospels, where
Jesus' confrontation with demons is prominent,
the New Testament does not have a great deal to
say about demons as such. This is perhaps a

warning to us not to be too preoccupied with
demons. They, no doubt, would like to have us
pay more attention to them, but it may be that
one of their more deceitful thrusts is to get us
to be thinking more about them than about the
Lord and obedience to him. Be that as it may
(I do not want to appear to be privy to the
counsels of demons), the New Testament does have
a great deal to say about evil, particularly in
its collective expression. Paul's wider terminology, and particularly what he says about
"principalities and powers," will be a way of
getting into some of these larger concerns which
are related to what we have found other authors
talking about when using the word "demon."

Nature of Demons

Paul's two references to demons indicate
that they are evil spiritual beings intent on
deceiving and leading astray human beings, either
through pagan religion or heretical versions of
Christianity. He, in common with the rest of
the New Testament, shows no interest in their
origin. When they came into existence and how
they became wicked is of no concern for the New
Testament authors. The interest of the New
Testament rather is in the actual situation of
the world and of Christians in it and the kind
of conduct necessary in view of the spiritual
realities of life.

Paul does see the evil spiritual forces as
subordinate to Satan and functioning as one

under his leadership. Otherwise, he pays no attention to the interrelationship of spiritual beings. In the passage read at the beginning, Ephesians refers to the "wiles of the devil" (6:11)[4] and to the "flaming darts of the evil one" (vs. 16), indicating the single head of the "principalities and powers" and warning again against his deceitfulness and the seriousness of his assaults against believers. Ephesians also describes the previous conduct of pagan converts to Christianity as "following the course of this world, following the prince of the power of the air, the spirit that is now at work in the sons of disobedience" (2:2). The powers thus have a prince;[5] their dwelling is the atmosphere around the earth, "heavenly" places. And their work is disobedience to God, which brings on a condition of spiritual death, because of trespasses and sins (Ephesians 2:1-3). The connection of the devil with actual physical death is made in a book not by Paul but for long associated with him, Hebrews 2:14:

> Since therefore the children share in flesh and blood, [Christ] himself likewise partook of the same nature, that through death he might destroy him who has the power of death, that is the devil, and deliver all those who through fear of death were subject to lifelong bondage.[6]

As in the Synoptic Gospels, so in Paul the devil is the tempter. He is intent on keeping mankind away from God and from eternal life.

"The god of this world has blinded the minds of the unbelievers, to keep them from seeing the light of the gospel of the glory of Christ, who is the likeness of God" (2 Corinthians 4:4).[7] This passage does not mean that human freedom is removed. Only unbelievers are blinded. And they do not have to remain unbelievers: "When a man turns to the Lord, the veil is removed" (2 Corinthians 3:16) and "It is the God who said, 'Let light shine out of darkness,' who has shone in our hearts to give the light of the knowledge of the glory of God in the face of Christ" (2 Corinthians 4:6). The recipients of Ephesians had changed; they "once walked" in sin, but God "made them alive" (Ephesians 2:1-3). Paul speaks further of the deceptive activity of Satan in a passage which says it is allowed by God, because men themselves refuse his truth:

> The coming of the lawless one by the activity of Satan will be with all power and with pretended signs and wonders, and with all wicked deception for those who are to perish, because they refused to love the truth and so be saved. Therefore God sends upon them a strong delusion, to make them believe what is false, so that all may be condemned who did not believe the truth but had pleasure in unrighteousness.
> (2 Thessalonians 2:9-12)

Such is the seriousness of being on the right side in the struggle between God and Satan and the importance of the right attitude--love of the truth versus pleasure in unrighteousness.

The Christian has special resources and

added assurances as he faces the devil's deceptions. "No temptation has overtaken you that is not common to man. God is faithful, and he will not let you be tempted beyond your strength, but with the temptation will also provide the way of escape" (1 Corinthians 10:13). Thus Paul says to Christians to "withstand" the evil one. Similarly, Peter warns: "Be sober, be watchful. Your adversary the devil prowls around like a roaring lion, seeking someone to devour. Resist him, firm in your faith" (1 Peter 5:8f.). And James says much the same, "Submit yourselves therefore to God. Resist the devil and he will flee from you. Draw near to God and he will draw near to you" (James 4:7f.).

The New Testament does not place responsibility for sin on the devil. The devil would have no power without human consent, for as James 1:14 explains, "Each person is tempted when he is lured and enticed by his own desire." Jesus taught that the evil thoughts which defile a man come from his own heart (Matthew 15:19). The devil may be viewed as the tempter, but there would be no temptation unless something within us responded to the appeal. To return to Ephesians, we by our emotions and attitudes "give opportunity to the devil" (Ephesians 4:27).

The necessity to be watchful and informed about the will of God is emphasized by the extreme cleverness of the devil and his demons. Paul warned against certain "false apostles, deceitful workmen" who disguised themselves as apostles of Christ, "And no wonder, for even Satan disguises himself as an angel of light. So it is not strange if his servants also disguise themselves as servants of righteousness" (2 Corinthians 11:13f.). A friend of mine told me that if he were looking for demons today, he would look in the pulpits of the land. That may unduly single out preachers, but it is a reminder that no place is immune from temptation and things are not always what they seem. Sin does try to find a home in churches and religious activities. It is a characteristic of evil to appear as attractive, not ugly: it is only as its real nature is exposed and its consequences brought to light that its true ugliness is evident.

In view of these warnings it is well to be reminded that the influence of temptation is limited. The Christian has a stronger armor; he is able to "stand."

Activities

The nature of the spiritual forces opposed to God which we have considered prepares us for further consideration of their activities according to the Pauline epistles. In Paul there is no mention of demon possession or of casting out demons, perhaps because he was writing to Christians, over whom demons had no such power. In contrast to the Gospels, Paul labels the opponents of Christ as cosmic powers and death,

and describes Christ's victory in terms of his
death and resurrection. Paul saw the activities
of the "principalities and powers" at work in
the government, in nature, and in religion.
These things--the state, the world, and religion
--were obviously created by God and intended for
good, but such is the capacity of the created
order for evil that these spheres could and did
become demonic.

Paul uses the terminology of "principalities
and powers" for the governmental authorities in
the state. Titus 3:1 tells Christians "to be
submissive to rulers and authorities," but the
words are the same as are translated "principalities and powers" elsewhere. Romans 13:1 says,
"Let every person be subject to the governing
authorities," again the word "authorities" is
the same as "powers." Both passages seem clearly
to have in mind the political authorities in the
state, but Paul's terminology elsewhere may
indicate he is including something more as well.
In Jewish thought each nation had an angel ruler
and guardian which personified it.[8] Paul may
have in mind these spiritual beings as well as
their human embodiments in officials and magistrates. Governmental authorities were
instituted by God for good (Romans 13:1-7), but
they may act wrongly, as we know all too well.

A striking example of action occurring on
two planes may be seen in regard to the crucifixion of Jesus. On the human level Jesus was put

to death by a conspiracy of the Jewish rulers
and the Roman governor. On another level the
"spiritual hosts of wickedness" were behind his
death. Paul says that he imparts a wisdom that
is not "of this age or of the rulers of this age,
who are doomed to pass away. But we impart a
secret and hidden wisdom of God, which God de-
creed before the ages for our glorification.
None of the rulers of this age understood this;
for if they had, they would not have crucified
the Lord of glory" (1 Corinthians 2:6-8). This
passage has sometimes been seen as a contra-
diction to the Gospels, where the demons did
recognize Jesus as "Lord of glory." However,
Paul does not say that the "rulers of this age"
did not know who Jesus really was. Rather, they
did not know God's wisdom, which was in his plan
before the ages. They did not understand that in
killing Christ they were losing their hold on
mankind.[9] They did not understand God's plan for
man's salvation.[10]

The "principalities and powers" are also
designated by Paul as "world rulers." As such
they stand behind the order of nature. "World
rulers" is a word used of the astral deities, or
stars and planets worshipped as gods. The
created world was affected by human sin in
Genesis 3, because part of the punishment on mankind involved a curse upon the ground that it
would produce thorns and be resistant to man's
labor so that he would produce his food with

sweat and toil (Genesis 3:17-19). Thus Paul
sees the redemption of the natural order bound
up with man's redemption:

> For the creation waits with eager
> longing for the revealing of the sons of
> God; for the creation was subjected to
> futility, not of its own will but by the
> will of him who subjected it in hope;
> because the creation itself will be set
> free from its bondage to decay and obtain
> the glorious liberty of the children of
> God. We know that the whole creation has
> been groaning in travail together until
> now; and not only the creation, but we our-
> selves, who have the first fruits of the
> Spirit, groan inwardly as we wait for
> adoption as sons, the redemption of our
> bodies. (Romans 8:19-23)

The promise of adoption as "sons of God"
(incidentally a phrase which refers to angels in
the Old Testament)[11] also figures in Galatians
4:1-10:

> I mean that the heir, as long as he is a
> child, is no better than a slave, though he
> is the owner of all the estate; but he is
> under guardians and trustees until the date
> set by the father. So with us; when we were
> children, we were slaves to the elemental
> spirits of the universe. But when the time
> had fully come, God sent forth his Son,
> born of woman, born under the law, to re-
> deem those who were under the law, so that
> we might receive adoption as sons. And be-
> cause you are sons, God has sent the Spirit
> of his Son into our hearts, crying, "Abba!
> Father!" So through God you are no longer
> a slave but a son, and if a son then an
> heir.
> Formerly, when you did not know God, you
> were in bondage to beings that by nature are
> no gods; but now that you have come to know
> God, or rather to be known by God, how can

> you turn back again to the weak and beg-
> garly elemental spirits, whose slaves you
> want to be once more? You observe days,
> and months, and seasons, and years. I am
> afraid I have labored over you in vain.

The term "elemental spirits" is ambiguous, but
Paul apparently includes the astral deities of
paganism and the spiritual forces behind the
natural order of the world which he sees pagans,
in some forms of their religion, worshipping.
These "elemental spirits" held mankind in bondage, and one expression of their control was
certain calendar observances. Either nature
religions or astrology or both could have been
included. Paul speaks of the "elements of the
world" also in Colossians 2:8, 20, where again
he relates these guiding principles of the universe to false religious practices: ascetic
regulations (2:21), worship of angels (2:18),
and observance of religious festivals (2:16).

Nature obviously was created good by God
(Genesis 1), but it shared in the curse for human
sin; and many things about nature, e.g. its de-
cay (Romans 8:21) and the disasters it inflicts
show its created state and demonic possibilities.

One dangerous perversion of both the state
and nature in Paul's day (but not confined to
it) was to make them an object of worship. This
was done in the emperor cult of Rome and in the
nature religions. These perversions show the
demonic possibilities of what is created good.
Even man's religious nature, and religion itself,

can oppose God and become an expression of the demonic. We have already seen how Paul treats idolatry as directed toward demons (1 Corinthians 10:20) and false doctrines as originating with demons (1 Timothy 4:1). The "principalities and powers" could even use God's law revealed through Moses in order to turn men from obedience to God to obedience to themselves. The striking thing about the passage from Galatians 4 quoted above is that Paul seems to put the law of Moses in some sense on the same level with pagan religion, so that the desire to impose the regulations of the law would be like returning to the regulations of pagan religion. Jews and pagans were both subjected to law given by angelic powers (Galatians 3:19; 4:1-11).[12] Both Jews and pagans had failed to see beyond their laws to the God who was creator and so made what was secondary and relative into an absolute. Such is a device of the demons. Sin thwarted God's purposes and kept man from humble obedience. So the religious sphere can be seized by forces opposed to God--whether by pagan gods, Jewish law, or Christian heresies.

In view of the demonic possibilities of government, nature, and religion, we should not look for salvation through political processes, through controlling nature (either by technological advancement or environmental improvement), or through human religion (either by education or improving the conscience). This is not to

make these things unimportant. It is only to
say that these things are always only relative
and insufficient of themselves. Wherein then do
we look for deliverance?

Victory in Christ

       Over against the state, the world, the law
and other forms of religion, Paul directs our
attention to Jesus Christ. Paul does not dwell
on the activities of the spiritual powers in the
world. He has more to say about their subordinate status and the superiority of Christ.

       All spiritual beings, apart from the God-
head himself, are created beings. And this
creation took place in Christ or by means of
him; and indeed all was created for him.

            For in him [Christ] all things were
            created, in heaven and on earth, visible
            and invisible, whether thrones or dominions
            or principalities or authorities [again, it
            is powers]--all things were created through
            him and for him. (Colossians 1:16)

And so, the "principalities and powers" are subjected to Christ by reason of creation. But at
some point these created spirits, or at least
some of them, became alienated from God and
failed to serve his purposes and thus became in
need of reconciliation. In other words, they
had been good beings, but they became bad. Not
only was creation accomplished through Christ,
but so was redemption. The blood shed on the
cross is the means of reconciliation even for the
angelic beings: Through Christ God reconciles

"to himself all things, whether on earth or in
heaven, making peace by the blood of his cross"
(Colossians 1:20).

The power of Christ over the heavenly
powers was shown at the cross. Colossians 2:15
has its difficulties in translation and interpretation. Although I am not particularly happy
with the RSV rendering, I shall stay with it
since I am not satisfied how to take the verse:
"He disarmed the principalities and powers and
made a public example of them, triumphing over
them in him." Whether the subject is God or
Christ, whether we say "disarming" or "stripping
off," whether the triumph was "in Christ" or "in
the cross," the various ways the verse may be
translated does not affect the point of utmost
importance, which we want to make here. The
principalities and powers have been defeated by
Christ. This defeat was connected with the can-
celling of the debt of sin at the cross (vs. 14).
The power of the world rulers over mankind is
the result of human sin. When our trespasses
are forgiven, the world rulers no longer have a
claim on human life. Christ's victory thus was
secured on the cross.

God vindicated Christ and confirmed his
place in the spiritual hierarchy by the resurrection. Paul's prayer for Christians is that they
might know

> what is the immeasurable greatness of
> God's power in us who believe, according

> to the working of his great might which he
> accomplished in Christ when he raised him
> from the dead and made him sit at his
> right hand in the heavenly places, far
> above all rule and authority [principality
> and power] and powers [authority] and
> dominion, and above every name that is
> named, not only in this age but also in
> that which is to come; and he has put all
> things under his feet and has made him the
> head over all things for the church, which
> is his body, the fulness of him who fills
> all in all. (Ephesians 1:19-23)

No power is greater than God's power, no authority is greater than God's authority; and that
power was exercised in raising Christ from the
dead, that authority was conferred on him,
making him supreme over all else; and that power
is available to believers and is at work in them.
There is no reason for them to be subject to
angelic beings or subservient to their require-
ments. 1 Peter 3:21f. echoes Paul's words,
"Baptism . . . now saves you . . . through the
resurrection of Jesus Christ, who has gone into
heaven and is at the right hand of God, with
angels, authorities, and powers subject to him."[13]

     The powers have been overcome by Christ,
yet the message of that victory has to be taken
everywhere. I remember that after the defeat of
Japan in World War II, there remained islands in
the Pacific where word of the surrender did not
reach until years later. Pockets of resistance,
where in effect the war was still going on, remained for a long time. Or, viewed from another

perspective, the strength of the powers, as we have seen, comes from human sin. As long as human beings choose to follow the powers, they have strength and influence. Christ has removed the power of sin in principle, but men have to accept him and his salvation for his triumph at the cross to be effective in their lives. Consequently, Paul also connects the work of Christ with the preaching of the Gospel.

> To me, though I am the very least of all the saints, this grace was given, to preach to the Gentiles the unsearchable riches of Christ, and to make all men see what is the plan of the mystery hidden for ages in God who created all things; that through the church the manifold wisdom of God might now be made known to the principalities and powers in the heavenly places. This was according to the eternal purpose which he has realized in Christ Jesus our Lord. (Ephesians 3:8-11)

This passage, particularly verse 10, has been used as a prooftext that the task of the church is to preach the gospel. Such is the work of the church, but this passage can be used to show that only by emphasis on verse 9 ("to make all men see what is the plan . . . of God") and not by verse 10. Those to whom the wisdom of God is revealed in verse 10 are the "principalities and powers," the angelic and spiritual hosts who are in "heavenly places." There have been some ambitious missionary plans made in the last century, but I am not aware of a team preparing a spaceship in order to go and preach to the angels.

Rather, the verse is saying that the church, the
embodiment of God's eternal purpose in Christ,
by its very existence as the new, redeemed
people of God, manifests to angels something
more than they formerly knew about God's mani-
fold wisdom.[14] That eternal purpose of God was
for all men to receive the unsearchable riches
of Christ. And so, as the gospel spreads, men
are delivered from the rule of the principalities and powers and come into the possession of
Christ.

As long as men spurn the gospel and sin
reigns in human hearts, the forces of evil have
a sphere of control. Therefore, only at the
second coming of Christ, when sin and death are
finally brought to an end, will the demonic
powers be completely defeated.

> For as in Adam all die, so also in Christ
> shall all be made alive. But each in his
> own order; Christ the first fruits, then at
> his coming those who belong to Christ.
> Then comes the end, when he delivers the
> kingdom to God the Father after destroying
> every rule and every authority and power
> [every principality, power, and dominion].
> For he must reign until he has put all his
> enemies under his feet. The last enemy to
> be destroyed is death. . . .
> When the perishable puts on the imperish-
> able, and the mortal puts on immortality,
> then shall come to pass the saying that is
> written:
> "Death is swallowed up in victory."
> "O death, where is thy victory?
> O death, where is thy sting?"
> The sting of death is sin, and the power
> of sin is the law. But thanks be to God,

> who gives us the victory through our Lord
> Jesus Christ. (1 Corinthians 15:22-26,
> 54-57)

Christ rules now. He will reign until all his
enemies are destroyed; the last one to be destroyed will be death. Christ's own resurrection was the guarantee of the victory over death.
His resurrection was the first fruits of the
harvest which promises the remainder of the harvest. When he comes again, there will be the
resurrection of those who belong to him. Then
comes the end when he delivers up the kingship
to God the Father. Every power opposed to God
will have been destroyed, and God will be all in
all. We know who will win in the end. The outcome is certain.

The perspective reflected in these passages
which describe a victory at the cross and
resurrection and yet ascribe it also to the
second coming has been called "inaugurated
eschatology." There is both a "now" and a "not
yet" to the Christian faith. Significant things
have been accomplished and significant blessings
are available now, but the fullness of these
things yet awaits the future. Oscar Cullmann
illustrated it by comparison to D-Day and V-Day
in World War II.[15] D-Day was the designation
for the landing of the allied troops on the
beaches of Normandy in France, beginning on June
6, 1944. The successful invasion of fortress
Europe sealed the outcome of the war against Nazi
Germany. There was no longer doubt about the

outcome. If the allied powers could success-
fully sustain an invasion force on the continent,
the eventual defeat of Germany must follow. A
lot of hard fighting ensued before the German
surrender brought on the celebration of V-Day,
Victory Day, on May 8, 1945. The first coming
of Christ was D-Day, the successful invasion of
enemy occupied earth by Christ. We could be
even more specific and say that D-Day was Death
Day. The second coming will be V-Day.

Another illustration would be that of a
"lame-duck" president. An office-holder whose
term of office is soon to expire, after a
successor has been chosen, in the period of time
before the new office-holder is inaugurated is
called a "lame-duck." He will not last much
longer. But during that time he has all the
authority of the office, and anything he does in
his official capacity is legally binding. The
devil is the "lame-duck" ruler of this world.
His term of office will soon be up. We do not
know the "times and seasons" which God has
appointed for finally removing him from power
and bringing the legitimate Ruler. In the mean-
time, of course, the devil can do a lot of
damage.

A friend of mine gave another illustration
of a different nature. He and his friends, when
growing up, were quite mischievous. This was in
the time when children could still go to the
movies unaccompanied by an adult. And at that

time Saturday morning was cartoon time at the movie theatres, and a favorite way for children in small towns to spend Saturdays was to watch the cartoons. This friend of mine and his buddies caught a large number of wasps and removed the stingers and kept them in jars for the time for the movie house to open. Then, before the lights went out for the cartoons to start, they released the wasps from the jars. No one else knew the stingers had been removed. There was more excitement than usual in the movie house in that small town that Saturday morning. The devil has had his stinger removed. "The sting of death is sin" (1 Corinthians 15:56). The power of sin has been broken by Christ. But the devil, like those wasps in the movie theatre, can still cause quite a bit of excitement in the world.

Again, we may think of a wild animal who has been wounded. He has received a mortal wound, a death-blow, but until he actually dies, the animal is very dangerous, indeed more dangerous than before the wound was inflicted. This may be seen as a biblical illustration of the condition of the devil, for Revelation 13:3 speaks of the beast with a mortal wound, only in that case the wound was healed. The devil has received a mortal wound from Christ; however, he is still extremely dangerous until the second coming of Christ.

The Victory of Christians

The reference in 1 Corinthians 15:23 to
"those who belong to Christ" who will be raised
at his second coming may serve to introduce the
thought that Christians share in the victory won
by Christ in his death and resurrection. "For
in him the whole fulness of deity dwells bodily,
and you have come to fulness of life in him, who
is the head of all rule and authority [princi-
pality and power]" (Colossians 2:10). At baptism
the believer is identified with Christ's death
and resurrection: "You were buried with him in
baptism, in which you were also raised with him
through faith in the working of God, who raised
him from the dead" (Colossians 2:12). At baptism the believer symbolically identifies with
the death of Christ which brings forgiveness of
sins and with the resurrection of Christ which
brings a new life.[16] By being baptized one ex-
presses his faith in the resurrection of Christ.
That resurrection was by the working or activity
of God, and to be buried and raised from the
water demonstrates faith in that powerful act of
God; and by identifying with that experience of
Christ we are identified with its power and
effects. Included in those benefits of baptism
are deliverance from the power and influence of
the spiritual beings opposed to God. "God has
delivered us from the dominion of darkness and
transferred us to the kingdom of his beloved
Son, in whom we have redemption, the forgiveness

of sins" (Colossians 1:13). Christ now rules one's life, not the devil, demons, and darkness. When sins are forgiven, the powers have no more hold on one's life. They have no control where the lordship of Christ is acknowledged.

> We are more than conquerors through him who loved us. For I am sure that neither death, nor life, nor angels, nor principalities, nor things present, nor things to come, nor powers, nor height, nor depth, nor anything else in all creation, will be able to separate us from the love of God in Christ Jesus our Lord. (Romans 8:37-39)

That does not mean, however, that all is easy. There is a continuous struggle demanded. As we have seen, in the interval between the two comings of Christ, Satan and his subordinates can cause a lot of excitement. There is a lot of hard fighting between D-Day and V-Day. Satan has the world, so he attacks the church. My father has often said that the reason there is so much meanness in the church is that the devil already has the rest of the world in his hippocket, so the church is the only place where he needs to work; hence he makes a special effort on Christians. That may help explain, but it does not exonerate, sin in churches.

As a result, the words of Ephesians 6 with which we began have their pertinence. Notice the weapons of the Christians' warfare against the spiritual hosts of wickedness. Those weapons are the truly spiritual qualities which correspond to the emphasis which Jesus gave in his

ministry (as considered in the first chapter).
The Christians' armor consists of truth,
righteousness, the gospel, faith, salvation, the
word of God, and prayer. This equipment is sup-
plied by God. It is God's truth, God's
righteousness, God's gospel, God's salvation,
God's word, the faith "once for all delivered"
which will sustain us. It is important to be
truthful, righteous, peaceful, believing, but
these things are insufficient to resist the evil
one. It is much more important to claim God's
truth and God's righteousness and God's word.
One way the person who is already a Christian
does so, is through prayer. Both prayer and the
word are related in this passage to the Holy
Spirit--"Sword of the Spirit" and "Pray in the
spirit" (Ephesians 6:17, 18). Paul even more
than the Gospels (Luke 11:13-26) emphasizes the
importance of the indwelling Spirit for the
Christian life.[17]

The certainty of Christians' victory is
perhaps indicated by an enigmatic statement in
1 Corinthians 6:3: "Do you not know that we are
to judge angels?" That puzzles me, because I
think of having to face judgment myself.[18] How
then can Christians judge angels? Do we join
with Christ, sharing his function of judge as we
share so much else with him? Or is our salvation
a judgment on disobedient angels?[19] Some disobedient angels are already under punishment.

> For if God did not spare the angels when
> they sinned, but cast them into Tartarus and

> committed them to pits of nether gloom to
> be kept until the judgment . . . then the
> Lord knows how to rescue the godly from
> trial, and to keep the unrighteous under
> punishment until the day of judgment.
> (2 Peter 2:4-9; cf. Jude 6)

This is a warning of what happens to the disobedient now, but the Christian has a different
prospect: "If we have died with him, we shall
also live with him; if we endure, we shall also
reign with him" (2 Timothy 2:11f.).

Johannine Literature

The Johannine literature does not offer new
concepts beyond those already encountered, but
its different wording will serve to enforce some
points already made. Moreover, it is worth including in order to give a more nearly complete
presentation of New Testament teaching. It is
especially in the book of Revelation that the
devil and demons occupy an important place.

Revelation reflects the popular view that
deserted areas are the haunt of demons (18:2).
The activities in which the devil and demons are
involved in the book of Revelation are those
which remained important in Christian literature
of the next two centuries: (1) The demonic
spirits deceive and perform spectacular signs
(16:4); (2) the demons were associated with
idols (9:20) and so pagan religion was a manifes-
tation of Satan (2:13); (3) Satan taught false
teachings (2:24); (4) the devil was behind the
persecution of Christians (2:10) and (as the

dragon) stood behind the secular power (the
beast), to which he gave his authority, and its
religious cultus (13:1-14; 19:19f.).

First John connects sin with the devil and
identifies the purpose in Jesus' coming as to
destroy his works: "He who commits sin is of
the devil; for the devil has sinned from the
beginning. The reason the Son of God appeared
was to destroy the works of the devil" (1 John
3:8). The Gospel of John associates this
destruction of the works of the devil with the
lifting up of Jesus in his death and resurrection: "Now is the judgment of this world, now
shall the ruler of this world be cast out; and
I, when I am lifted up from the earth, will draw
all men to myself" (John 12:31). This apparently is what is described in vivid pictorial terms
in Revelation 12:7-12:

> Now war arose in heaven, Michael and his
> angels fighting against the dragon; and the
> dragon and his angels fought, but they were
> defeated and there was no longer any place
> for them in heaven. And the great dragon
> was thrown down, that ancient serpent, who
> is called the Devil and Satan, the deceiver
> of the whole world--he was thrown down to
> the earth, and his angels were thrown down
> with him. And I heard a loud voice in
> heaven, saying, "Now the salvation and
> power and the kingdom of our God and the
> authority of his Christ have come, for the
> accuser of our brethren has been thrown
> down, who accuses them day and night before
> our God. And they have conquered him by
> the blood of the Lamb and by the word of
> their testimony, for they loved not their

> lives even unto death. Rejoice then, O
> heaven and you that dwell therein! But woe
> to you, O earth and sea, for the devil has
> come down to you in great wrath, because
> he knows that his time is short!"

The binding, loosing, and final destruction of
Satan are described in Revelation 20.[20]

The overthrow of Satan by Christ, his violent resistance while in his death throes, and
his final destruction are important themes in
the book of Revelation. For a short time he has
dominion over the earth, and he does his best to
make a hell of it (Revelation 13:7); but the
Lamb conquers him (17:14).[21] The efforts of the
devil and his angels make this life a time of
struggle for the saints of God. The means by
which they overcome is most significant: "They
have conquered him by the blood of the Lamb and
by the word of their testimony, for they loved
not their lives even unto death" (Revelation
12:11). They overcame by the blood of the Lamb,
the sacrificial atonement for sin made by Jesus;
by the word of their testimony (either the word
of God or their confession of that word); and by
dying to self (martyrdom or the willingness to
be martyrs).

First John gives further assurance to
Christians. "For whatever is born of God overcomes the world; and this is the victory that
overcomes the world, our faith. Who is it that
overcomes the world but he who believes that
Jesus is the Son of God?" (1 John 5:4).

"Little children, you are of God, and have overcome them [spirits of falsehood]; for he who is
in you is greater than he who is in the world"
(1 John 4:4). We return perhaps here to the
theme of the indwelling Spirit who is superior
to the spirits of the devil and of the world.

Demons Today

It is now time to apply our historical and
biblical studies to the contemporary world. Are
there demons today? If so, what do they do?
There are at least four possible approaches
which might be taken: (1) Demons never existed.
The New Testament language represents an accomo-
dation to the beliefs of the time and was a way
of talking about another reality. (2) Demons
exist and are still active in all of the same
ways in which they were in New Testament times.
The New Testament describes a literal reality
that is a permanent part of human existence.
(3) The demons existed, but were so defeated or
even destroyed by the ministry of Jesus and his
disciples that they are not active now. They
were allowed a special period of activity around
the first century in order that the person and
power of Jesus might be magnified. (4) The
demons still exist, but their power is limited.

Each of these views is possible, and each
has had its supporters. For myself I find it
hard to accept the accommodation theory. Idolatry too was part of the structure of things in
New Testament times, but Jesus and the apostles

did not accommodate their language to popular belief here but plainly said it was wrong. I find it easier to believe that demons are a literal reality and still exist. To believe in a personal force of evil is no more difficult than to believe in a personal God and his angels. On the other hand, to grant to demons the full exercise of the power they demonstrated in New Testament times would seem to say that the coming of Christ has not made any difference in the cosmic situation. So I would have difficulty in the view that our situation now is no different from that of the first century. Neither, however, can I go so far as to say that demonic activity was confined to the first century. There seems no difference in the nature of the reports from the second and third centuries from those of the first century. And contemporary reports of demonic activity in pagan countries of the world seem strikingly similar to ancient reports. I confess, however, that I am not knowledgeable in this area of anthropology and have not made a special study of the reports, but am relying on the evidence of others. Taken altogether, therefore, I conclude that the fourth alternative is the correct one. There were demons, and there still are demons, but their powers are limited and their final destruction is certain. In what ways they are limited, or what are the differences between their activities now and in the time before the coming of Christ, I

confess ignorance, because I have not found such
information spelled out in the New Testament. I
would be glad to receive further instruction on
this subject. But there are things which have
emerged from our study which I consider in-
finitely more important than determination of
these speculative matters. Some things are true
whatever we conclude about the activity of demons today, or even about their existence.

My studies of ancient demonology have left
me with many unanswered questions. I have
hesitated even to offer the opinions which I just
now have. Although I have not learned as much
about demons as I would like to know, and you
would like to know, I have learned much more
about Christ; otherwise I would begrudge the
time spent studying about demons. What I do
know--and what is a far more important con-
sideration--is the Christian conviction that
such powers have been defeated by Christ and
hold no threat for the Christian unless he sur-
renders to them.

Conclusions

I shall attempt my summary by means of an
alliteration on the letter D, for the demons.

(1) The demons are not divine. They are
created (Colossians 1:16). As all of God's
creation, they were created good, but at some
time and for reasons we do not know they became
bad.

(2) The demons became disobedient (Jude 6;

2 Peter 2:4), even as human beings were created good but chose rebellion and disobedience. The demonic or the potential for the demonic is part of the structure of the created order, so is still with us.

(3) The demons dominate the world outside of Christ (2 Corinthians 4:4; Ephesians 2:2; John 14:30; 1 John 5:19). There is something evil at work in the world--something superhuman and opposed to God.

(4) The work of demons is to deceive and to destroy. Having disobeyed God, they seek to tempt men to follow their path (Matthew 4:1ff.; John 8:44; 2 Corinthians 2:11; 11:14f.; 2 Thessalonians 2:9; Hebrews 2:14).

(5) The demons are dependent on sin. The source of their power is ultimately human beings themselves (Ephesians 4:7; 1 Corinthians 7:5; 2 Corinthians 4:4).

(6) Christ has defeated the demonic powers (Colossians 2:15), so they are delimited in their power and sphere of operations.

(7) The demons will themselves ultimately be destroyed (Matthew 25:41; Revelation 12:9; 20:10).

(8) The divine Spirit, God's own Holy Spirit, is God's answer to the spiritual vacuum in our lives (Galatians 5:16ff.).

(9) The Christian faith dispels constant fear of evil. It bears witness to the triumph of Christ (Colossians 2:20ff.).

(10) The <u>desire</u> to obey God and to live the
Christian life is evidence that one has passed
from darkness to light and from death to life
(1 John 1:7ff.; 3:10, 14, 23).

Since this chapter has primarily concerned
Pauline material, Paul should have the final
word:

> Have this mind among yourselves, which
> you have in Christ Jesus, who, though he
> was in the form of God, did not count
> equality with God a thing to be grasped,
> but emptied himself, taking the form of a
> servant, being born in the likeness of men.
> And being found in human form he humbled
> himself and became obedient unto death,
> even death on a cross. Therefore God has
> highly exalted him and bestowed on him the
> name which is above every name, that at
> the name of Jesus every knee should bow, in
> heaven and on earth and under the earth,
> and every tongue confess that Jesus Christ
> is Lord, to the glory of God the Father.
> (Philippians 2:5-11)

All must eventually acknowledge Christ and bow
in obedience to him: demons as well as men. Is
it not better to confess him as Lord now?

Notes

[1] For this chapter I am particularly in-
debted to G. B. Caird, Principalities and Powers:
A Study in Pauline Theology (Oxford, 1956);
Heinrich Schlier, Principalities and Powers in
the New Testament (New York: Herder and Herder,
1961); G. H. C. MacGregor, "Principalities and
Powers: The Cosmic Background of Paul's
Thought," New Testament Studies 1 (1954) 17-28;
cf. also John J. Gunther, St. Paul's Opponents
and Their Background (Leiden: Brill, 1973), pp.
172-208, 271-297. The interpretive framework
adopted in this chapter is denied by Wesley
Carr, Angels and Principalities (Cambridge:
Cambridge University Press, 1981); the tenden-
tious nature of his argument is shown by the
fact that so impossible is it to fit Ephesians
6:12 into his position that he must regard it as
a second-century interpolation--pp. 104-110.

[2] Cf. Deuteronomy 32:17; Isaiah 65:11. See
chapters II and III.

[3] E.g. Testament of Levi 3:8; 1 Enoch 61:10f.

[4] Cf. 2 Timothy 2:26.

[5] Cf. the discussion of Luke 11:17ff. in
chapter I.

[6] Cf. Wisdom of Solomon 2:24. The "angel of
death" occurs in rabbinic literature in such
passages as bAboda Zara 20b; Midrash Rabbah,
Genesis 9:10. The Testament of Abraham 16ff.
personifies death, who explains to Abraham that
he comes to the righteous in beauty and gentle-
ness but to the wicked in ugliness and bitter-
ness.

[7] Cf. Ascension of Isaiah 2:4, "For the
prince of unrighteousness who rules this world
is Beliar."

[8] Deuteronomy 32:8f.; Daniel 10:13; 12:1;
Sirach 17:17.

[9]G. B. Caird, op. cit., chapter 4.

[10]Cf. 1 Peter 1:12; Ephesians 3:10.

[11]Job 1:6; Psalms 89:6.

[12]Caird, op. cit., chapter 2.

[13]Cf. Hebrews 10:12f.

[14]Cf. 1 Peter 1:10.

[15]Oscar Cullmann, Christ and Time (Philadelphia: Westminster, 1950) pp. 84, 141.

[16]Cf. Romans 6:3-5.

[17]Galatians 5:16ff.; 1 Corinthians 6:19; Galatians 4:6; 2 Timothy 1:14; Romans 8:9-11.

[18]Matthew 25:31ff.; 2 Corinthians 5:10; Revelation 20:11ff.

[19]Matthew 12:41f.

[20]If one asks how Satan can be bound yet "prowl around like a roaring lion" (1 Peter 5:8), we can think of a wild animal on a leash-- dangerous within the sphere where it can move about but limited by the length of the leash.

[21]Regnar Leivestad, Christ the Conqueror (New York: Macmillan, 1954), section III.7.

Bibliography

Bamberger, B. J. _Fallen Angels_. Philadelphia:
Jewish Publication Society, 1952.

Bietenhard, H. "Air, Demon, Cast Out." _The
New International Dictionary of New
Testament Theology_, ed. Colin Brown.
Vol. I. Grand Rapids: Zondervan, 1975.

Brown, Peter. "Sorcery, Demons, and the Rise of
Christianity from Late Antiquity into the
Middle Ages." _Witchcraft, Confessions,
and Accusations_, ed. Mary Douglas.
London: Tavistock, 1970.

Caird, G. B. _Principalities and Powers: A
Study in Pauline Theology_. Oxford, 1956.

Carr, Wesley. _Angels and Principalities_.
Cambridge: Cambridge University Press,
1981.

Chalk, John Allen, et. al. _The Devil, You Say?_
Austin: Sweet, 1974.

Colpe, C. et. al. "Geister (Dämonen)."
Reallexikon für Antike und Christintum,
ed. Th. Klauser. Vol. IX. Stuttgart,
1976.

Eitrem, S. _Some Notes on the Demonology of the
New Testament. Section edition_. Oslo,
1966.

Foerster, W. "Daimōn, daimonion." _Theological
Dictionary of the New Testament_, ed.
G. Kittel. Vol. II. Grand Rapids:
Eerdmans, 1964.

Gokey, F. X. _The Terminology for the Devil and
Evil Spirits in the Apostolic Fathers_.
Washington: Catholic University Press,
1961.

Hiers, R. H. "Satan, Demons, and the Kingdom of
God." _Scottish Journal of Theology_.
27 (1974) 35-47.

Kallas, James. _Jesus and the Power of Satan_.
Philadelphia: Westminster, 1968.

_____. _The Real Satan_. Minneapolis:
Augsburg, 1975.

177

Kallas, James. The Satanward View: A Study in
    Pauline Theology. Philadelphia:
    Westminster, 1966.

Kelly, H. A. The Devil, Demonology, and
    Witchcraft. Garden City: Doubleday,
    1974.

Langston, Edward. Good and Evil Spirits.
    London: SPCK, 1942.

_____. Essentials of Demonology: A Study
    of Jewish and Christian Doctrine, Its
    Origin and Development. London:
    Epworth, 1949.

Leivestad, Ragnar. Christ the Conqueror: Ideas
    of Conflict and Victory in the New
    Testament. New York: Macmillan, 1954.

Ling, Trevor. The Significance of Satan: New
    Testament Demonology and its Contemporary
    Relevance. London: SPCK, 1961.

MacGregor, G. H. C. "Principalities and Powers:
    The Cosmic Background of Paul's Thought."
    New Testament Studies I (1954) 17-28.

McCasland, S. V. By the Finger of God. New
    York: Macmillan, 1951.

Montgomery, John Warwick. ed. Demon Possession:
    A Medical, Historical, Anthropological,
    and Theological Symposium. Minneapolis:
    Bethany Fellowship, 1976.

Newport, John P. Demons, Demons, Demons.
    Nashville: Broadman, 1972.

Owen, E. C. E. "Daimon and Cognate Words,"
    Journal of Theological Studies 32 (1931)
    133-153.

Reicke, Bo. The Disobedient Spirits and
    Christian Baptism: Study of 1 Peter
    III.19 and its Context. Copenhagen, 1946.

Russell, J. B. Satan: The Early Christian
    Tradition. Ithaca: Cornell, 1981.

Schlier, Heinrich. Principalities and Powers in
    the New Testament. New York: Herder and
    Herder, 1961.

Smith, J. Z. "Towards Interpreting Demonic Powers in Hellenistic and Roman Antiquity," <u>Aufstieg</u> und <u>Niedertang</u> der <u>Römischen</u> <u>Welt</u>, ed. H. Temporini and W. Haase. Vol. 16.2. Berlin: Walter de Gruyter, 1978.

Unger, Merrill F. <u>Biblical</u> <u>Demonology</u>. Wheaton: Scripture Press, 1952.

SYMPOSIUM SERIES